ALSO BY BONNIE KRISTIAN

A Flexible Faith: Rethinking What It Means to Follow Jesus Today

Untrustworthy: The Knowledge Crisis Breaking Our Brains, Polluting Our Politics, and Corrupting Christian Community

IN DEFENSE OF EVANGELICALISM

IN DEFENSE OF EVANGELICALISM

A Response to Its Cultured Despisers

BONNIE KRISTIAN

FORUM BOOKS

Forum Books
An imprint of the Penguin Random House Christian Publishing Group,
a division of Penguin Random House LLC
1745 Broadway, New York, NY 10019
forumconservativebooks.com
penguinrandomhouse.com

Library of Congress Cataloging-in-Publication Data
Names: Kristian, Bonnie author
Title: In defense of Evangelicalism / Bonnie Kristian.
Description: First edition. | New York, NY : Forum Books, 2026 |
Includes bibliographical references.
Identifiers: LCCN 2026015987 (print) | LCCN 2026015988 (ebook) |
ISBN 9798217153176 hardcover | ISBN 9798217153183 ebook
Subjects: LCSH: Evangelicalism--United States--History--21st century |
United States—Church history—21st century
Classification: LCC BR1642.U5 K75 2026 (print) |
LCC BR1642.U5 (ebook)
LC record available at https://lccn.loc.gov/2026015987
LC ebook record available at https://lccn.loc.gov/2026015988

Printed in the United States of America

1st Printing

The authorized representative in the EU for product safety and compliance is Penguin Random House Ireland, Morrison Chambers, 32 Nassau Street, Dublin D02 YH68, Ireland. https://eu-contact.penguin.ie

Bookmaking Team: Production editor: Jocelyn Kiker · Managing editor: Julia Wallace · Production manager: Mark Maguire · Copy editor: Andrew Buss · Proofreaders: Debbie Anderson, Julia Henderson

Book design by Diane Hobbing

For details on special quantity discounts for bulk purchases, contact specialmarketscms@penguinrandomhouse.com.

To my mother,
so evangelical she didn't know it

O Lord, our heavenly Father, almighty and everlasting God, you have brought us safely to the beginning of this day: Defend us by your mighty power, that we may not fall into sin nor run into any danger; and that, guided by your Spirit, we may do what is righteous in your sight; through Jesus Christ our Lord. Amen.

The Book of Common Prayer, 2019

FOREWORD

When I was a new Christian, in 1978, living in my hometown of Birmingham, Alabama, I attended a weeklong series of talks about Christian holiness given by pastors associated with something called the Keswick movement. It says a great deal about evangelicalism that the Keswick movement was started by an Anglican and a Quaker, and these sessions were being hosted by a Presbyterian church. Evangelicalism since its origin has crossed denominational and institutional borders. I vividly remember being quite taken with a recommendation made by one of the speakers: to begin a prayer with the confession, "Lord, I am the failure you always knew I would be."

This church had a small bookstore, and as in those days I could not (as in these days I cannot) pass an open bookstore without entering it, I browsed for a while and came away with two volumes. One was by an author I had heard of but not read: C. S. Lewis's *Mere Christianity.* The other, published by a firm with the peculiar name of Eerdmans, was a commentary on the book of Romans by a man named F. F. Bruce.

I enjoyed Lewis's book, but Bruce's commentary on Romans made a *far* greater impact on me at that time. What struck me with particular force was the ease and comfort with which Bruce connected the biblical text to the broader Hellenistic intellectual world, full of pagan philosophers and poets, in which the new Christian movement came to be. I learned with some bemusement but also excitement that one could be devoted to the authority of Scripture, as Bruce evidently was, and yet interested in and knowledgeable about non-biblical culture, as Bruce also evidently was.

Many years later I would learn that Bruce had grown up in Scotland in a very theologically conservative sect called the Plymouth Brethren, but his father, an itinerant evangelist, had encouraged his brilliant son to study classics. Indeed, Bruce was a classicist before becoming a biblical scholar—thus his comfort with a wide range of texts in Greek and Latin alike. But at the time all I knew was that my curiosity was piqued, and I began openly to consider something that had been worrying me in some recess of my mind. I was in college at the time, studying English literature and history, and I very much wanted to keep studying both of them when I graduated—but was an academic life possible for someone who really wanted to follow Jesus? The examples of Bruce and Lewis suggested it was not out of the question, but I wasn't sure.

Shortly thereafter I visited another church, this one a Bible church. ("Bible" was right there in its name!) A visiting apologist for the Christian faith was going to speak, and I wanted to hear what he had to say. I must admit that I do not remember what he *did* say, but that's because throughout his talk I thought about how to formulate the question I wanted to ask him if I got the chance. At the end I stood in line with other enthusiasts, and when I finally got to him I stammered out my concern: Could I be an academic *and* a faithful Christian?

Not only *could* I, he said, but the world desperately needed thoughtful Christians to be a presence—salt and light—in the secular academy. That said, he continued, it was important for me to take my scholarly work very seriously, for Christians who did not make the best use of their intellectual gifts, who settled for mediocrity, could end up being less than mediocre and could bring shame to the name of Christ. Therefore I should follow the advice of Ecclesiastes 9:10: "Whatever your hand finds to do, do it with all your might."

Six years later I interrupted work on my doctoral dissertation at the University of Virginia to take a one-year position at the "flagship" evangelical school, Wheaton College in Illinois—and that one year turned into twenty-nine. How my colleagues and students at Wheaton helped me grow to spiritual *and* intellectual maturity is a story for another day, but one event is worth noting: When my wife and I had a son, one of his first babysitters, a student of mine, turned out to be the daughter of the very apologist who had encouraged me to pursue an academic vocation as a follower of Jesus.

When I visited that Presbyterian church in Birmingham in 1978, I didn't know the word *evangelical*. But I had unwittingly walked right into a vast and complex Christian renewal movement that ended up shaping my life in utterly foundational ways and continues to shape it to this day.

"Ah yes," some might say, "you were lucky enough to encounter evangelicalism at its best. But what about when it's at its *worst*?" Well, I know a few things about that too, stories I will not tell here because Bonnie Kristian tells other stories very much like them in the book you're holding. But perhaps I should note this: That apologist for the Christian faith who encouraged me to pursue an academic calling—*and* warned me of the terrible possibility of bringing "shame to the name of Christ"—was Ravi Zacharias, who after his death in 2020 was revealed to have been a long-time serial sexual adventurer, exploiter, and predator, and who also diverted funds from his ministry to support his predation. When I learned about this I was horrified and disgusted, and filled with grief for his family; but even so, my debt to him cannot be canceled or forgotten. I must hold the two radically opposing truths in my mind at once: that this man was a terrible sinner and that he was the person God used to set me on a path that has brought me deep personal satisfaction and at least some measure of success.

In one sense all Bonnie Kristian is asking of her readers is to hold multiple truths about evangelicalism in mind: Consider, please, the whole truth and nothing but the truth, rather than clutching desperately to whatever confirms your prejudices and jettisoning or ignoring the rest. The psychiatrist and blogger Scott Alexander has written eloquently about the human tendency to make "isolated demands for rigor": raising your standards for proof when someone has made a claim you don't want to believe, and then lowering them when the claim in question is one you'd prefer to find true. There are also isolated demands for *virtue:* depending on whether you like or dislike a group, one bad apple may be just one bad apple, or it may be declared typical of the whole barrel.

Reaching the conclusion you want to reach is made easier by humans' difficulty dealing with the *scale* at which information is processed in the internet era: If in your social media feed you see dozens of rotten apples, you will believe that that tells you something definitive about the barrel, and that opinion is unlikely to change even when someone tells you that the barrel holds millions of apples. And if you are writing an article or book about a group you don't like, and you are unfortunate enough to have an editor who shares your hostility—which almost always happens to people who write about evangelicals—

you won't get the pushback you need to make your article or book a good one.

An evangelical writer responding in these conditions can only hope to overcome these cognitive distortions by gathering a great deal of information, assessing that information fairly, freely acknowledging the points rightly made by critics, and pushing back patiently but insistently on bad reasoning and bad (or badly interpreted) evidence. And that's what Bonnie Kristian does in this book. I couldn't have managed it—I lack the patience—so I am very glad that Kristian has done it for me.

I'm glad because, in spite of everything—and if you don't know what I mean by "everything," this book will tell you—I remain an evangelical. One of the people Kristian interviews says of evangelicals, "They are my people." Well, they are my people also, because they brought me out of a dark place—what that proto-evangelical John Bunyan called the Slough of Despond—and up to a higher ground where the sun shines on the green grass. Almost all that's good about me comes from my immersion in the world of evangelicalism, and I must honor my sisters and brothers in the faith for all they've done for me. Yes, sometimes—well, *often*—they drive me nuts, and when they do so in the future, as they certainly will, and when I start to forget the debts I owe them, as *I* certainly will, I'll have this book to help me remember what's what. Thanks, Bonnie Kristian: Now I'm in *your* debt.

Alan Jacobs

CONTENTS

INTRODUCTION

EVANGELICALISM IS A favorite whipping boy of American public life, and it has been throughout living memory.

In 1956, the inaugural editorial of *Christianity Today*—the movement's flagship magazine—described evangelicalism as "neglected, slighted, misrepresented."[1] And people within the movement aren't alone in recognizing this pattern.[2]

A few decades later, the conservative politician Barry Goldwater warned of evangelicals: "Mark my word, if and when these preachers get control of the [Republican] party, it's going to be a terrible damn problem. Frankly, these people frighten me."[3]

By the early 2000s, claims that evangelical voters' loyalty to then President George W. Bush meant looming theocracy and fascism were paired with routine mockery.[4] "On the tree of wacky media subjects, evangelical Christians are usually seen as the lowest-hanging fruit," the Jewish magazine *Tablet* sympathetically observed in 2008.[5] Not just politically troublesome or threatening but tacky, ignorant, backwards, stupid—an embarrassing American subculture always good for a laugh from our betters.[6]

Even when politically ascendant—as under the Reagan, George W. Bush, and Trump administrations—evangelicals remain on the outs in high culture, among the tastemakers and the educated elite. The Supreme Court has had no evangelical justice in my lifetime, and there is no other religious group that can be so safely skewered on TV. When an evangelical does climb to a position of secular power, we pass around the good news with a telling excitement: *Did you know he's a Christian? Yes, that guy! One of us.*

And I do mean *us:* I was raised in American evangelicalism. My mother was born again in adulthood, and she's never lost the convert's zeal. We were in church whenever the doors were open. I attended Christian schools we really couldn't afford. My very name is evangelical: *Kristian* is a deliberate variant of *Christian,* legally changed from another surname before my birth. When my mom decided she was in, she was *in.*

As for me, I never left.

I'D BEEN WORKING in journalism for about two years when Donald Trump announced his candidacy in 2015. I was in seminary, getting a theological master's degree at an evangelical school and building a journalism career at the same time. These days I work at *Christianity Today,* but back then I'd recently taken a gig as a news writer for an outlet called *The Week.* Editors there had realized that while their opinion team was ideologically diverse, the news team was populated with twentysomething Democrats with the cultural and religious habits that description suggests. They asked around for a young writer who could mix things up, and they found me.

The Week hired me for my politics, but my faith soon came in handy too. I was the only visibly practicing evangelical on the writing staff, and story assignments about evangelicalism began to flow my way. I pitched these stories too, because I felt I could cover them with confidence and offer insights our other writers might not reach.

Then came Trump. Like many educated evangelicals,[7] especially in the media, I was immediately put off by him at every level: morally, theologically, politically, aesthetically.[8] I never considered voting for Hillary Clinton (or, later, Joe Biden or Kamala Harris), but I was dismayed at Trump's clumsy pandering to evangelical voters and even more dismayed when it worked. That year and in the years to come, I wrote often about Trump and evangelicals, thinking through how it could be that *we* were so linked to *him* in the public mind.

I'm still dismayed, to be honest. Though I've come to hold that dismay in tension with the reality that many evangelicals have defensible, understandable reasons for their Trump votes, this isn't a book about how I learned to stop worrying and love the Donald.

It's about this larger problem with evangelicalism's place in the American public square—this long practice of uncharitable and inaccurate critique, now escalated to a point of frenzy by false conflation of the whole evangelical tradition with white evangelical representation in the Trump voting bloc.

It's not that we should be exempt from frank, even tough critique. Rather, many in the mainstream commentariat—and particularly "exvangelicals" writing for secular audiences—wildly miss the mark. Their accusations are contradictory and ungenerous, in some cases outright ignorant, manipulative, or unjust. Much of what they take as evidence of evangelical malevolence or threat is truly pretty mundane stuff—and often not unique to evangelicals but common to Christians across centuries and cultures, to Americans across political proclivities, or to fallen, finite humanity as a whole.

Worse, much of what these critics present as benevolent calls for reform functionally treat evangelicalism as a failed movement, irredeemable and embarrassing and without moral or spiritual credibility.[9] They introduce themselves as the remodel team, then announce it's a teardown.

THIS KIND OF criticism isn't new, of course. We felt "neglected, slighted, misrepresented" in the 1950s, recall, an era remembered with only some exaggeration as a time of record Christian religiosity in America.[10] As far back as 1925, journalist H. L. Mencken could casually assert that "evangelical Christianity, as everyone knows, is founded upon hate." And that line came in the course of describing a prominent evangelical as "a peasant come home to the dung-pile," a man possessed of "a childish theology, full of an almost pathological hatred of all learning, all human dignity, all beauty, all fine and noble things."[11]

But criticism of evangelicals has undeniably intensified since around 2015, during a decade when the rise of Trump coincided with the exvangelical phenomenon, including widespread public renunciations of evangelicalism; with rapid changes in American norms and laws around sex and gender; with a string of high-profile evangelical scandals; and with rising ignorance of religion in general.

Evangelicals were long since weird, outré, too into all that Jesus stuff. Still, in these recent years, the conversation really took a turn. It's unremarkable, now, to see sweeping, merciless, uncurious declarations from fellow Christians about white evangelicals' supposedly total corruption[12] and our individual responsibility for every evil Trump commits.[13]

Looking back, I'm not sure when I began to notice that something was off in the way evangelicals were being widely discussed. Journalists always want to be the first to a story, but

I can't claim to be first to this one—not least because the Trump-evangelicals relationship for a long time struck me as the more novel and pressing problem.

By 2018, though, I was pairing critique of evangelical alliances to Trump with swipes at progressive exvangelical double standards. In an article at *The Week,* I went after an exvangelical "suggestion that abortion and same-sex relationships are inappropriate topics for politics, and [that] evangelicals should keep publicly silent on these points lest they create 'an American theocracy.'"[14]

But the first time I remember consciously objecting to this entire genre of criticism came in 2022, when I read *Jesus and John Wayne,* the extraordinarily successful 2020 volume from historian Kristin Kobes Du Mez. The argument of the book, as the subtitle puts it, is that "white evangelicals corrupted a faith and fractured a nation," but most of the word count is given over to history.

I finished *Jesus and John Wayne* with two impressions that I wasn't sure how to reconcile. On the one hand, so far as I knew personally and could gather from various reviews of the book, the historical work was detailed and competent, the writing compelling, and many of the stories Du Mez recounted exactly as disturbing as she said.

On the other hand, I couldn't recognize the debased movement Du Mez described. Her evidence seemed sound, so far as it went, but did the conclusion follow? The evangelicals I knew weren't corrupting our faith or fracturing our nation—at least, not any more than other Americans participating in our no-win politics. And that was true even of the white evangelicals, the Trump-voting evangelicals, the evangelicals with whom I had serious theological and political differences.

If you're in the pew at a good evangelical church every

week, you probably feel this same dissonance. As Protestants, we want to be open to calls to reform. As Christians, we want to respond to invitations for repentance. But the widespread monstering of evangelicalism just does not comport with the ordinary faithfulness we see each Sunday.

I can certainly think of plenty of counterexamples. Like any movement on this scale, evangelicalism has its freaks and fringes. There are any number of prominent figures, people with big churches (or at least big beards and big podcasts) with downright abhorrent beliefs and behavior. It's not hard to find these folks, nor is it wrong to want to avoid any association with them.

I'm not talking about them, though. I'm talking about the millions of people who make up ordinary American evangelicalism, people who are overwhelmingly kind and faithful, with normal (which is to say: low) levels of political engagement and expertise. They don't want their church[15] or their identity[16] to be focused on politics; they want both to be focused on Christ.

They're sincerely trying to bring their faith to bear in a fast-moving, polarized, two-party system with no good options.[17] It doesn't always go so well. But they are trying to follow Jesus, and they are trying to do the right thing. They do not merit contempt.

"AMERICANS DESERVE A fuller accounting of evangelicalism's role in our country's life," another Trump-critical historian, John Fea, wrote at *The Atlantic* in 2024 in response to *Jesus and John Wayne* and works like it.

"By focusing solely on the moments when evangelicals behave badly, we miss the way most evangelicals practice their faith," he continued. "Every day, you can find evangelicals serving their neighbors, addressing injustice, promoting the common good, and doing the things necessary to keep American democracy strong and compassionate."[18]

Fea's description—not naïve about evangelicalism's foibles and sins nor ignorant of its history, yet attentive to its real and distinctive goods—is one I *do* recognize. The fuller accounting he seeks is what this book aims to provide. It is a defense of evangelicalism because evangelicalism is worth defending.

My contention isn't that evangelicalism is perfect, merely that it is good. Its core emphases and practices, deep sincerity, and high enthusiasm are gifts to the church universal. American evangelicals do not need to "discern" new beliefs, repudiate all our history, or give up our tradition.

I don't say that lightly or reflexively or because I'm ignoring the headlines or dismissing stories of evangelical wrongs. There are ways in which evangelicalism *does* need reform. Our relationship to digital technology is currently high on my personal list of complaints. But that reform is not only *needed* but *deserved.* That is, evangelicalism is worth fixing. It deserves to be repaired, not discarded, and certainly not reduced to a tool in the hands of progressive pundits and populist politicians. And real reform of evangelicalism will make it *more* itself, not less, contrary to what its critics seem to wish.

In the eighteenth century, when evangelicalism as we now know it was developing on the revival circuit in England and America, evangelicals used "serious" as a kind of shibboleth. To ask if someone was serious was to ask if she was fervent in her faith, devoted to the Christian life and ethic, diligent in knowing Scripture, and thoughtfully seeking to follow Christ.[19]

This kind of seriousness is what American evangelicalism needs. But then, it is what every Christian needs and has always needed. The basic nature of the Christian life is that we have not "already obtained all this," as the apostle Paul wrote, but that we "press on to take hold of that for which Christ Jesus took hold" of us.[20]

IN THE CHAPTERS to come, Trump will inevitably make appearances, but this book is not about him. It's not an attempt to adjudicate evangelical support of Trump once and for all, because a central point is that evangelicalism can't be conflated with Trump votes. Highlighting that record is not the kill shot our critics suppose. It doesn't prove that evangelicals are a fundamentalist fifth column, nothing but hypocritical opportunists or manipulable rubes. Votes for Donald Trump are neither the whole of the evangelical project nor its invalidation.

So here's what you can expect instead. I'll examine five charges commonly leveled against American evangelicals, engaging what I take to be the strongest and most influential expositions of these ideas from recent years. Some accusations I'll roundly reject. They're not credible or reasonable, and they're out of touch with the reality found in churches across America. With others I'll find significant agreement alongside important caveats.

Before we come to any of that, though, a little scene-setting is in order. *Evangelical,* after all, is a contested term, notoriously difficult to explain to universal satisfaction. "It's an impossible job to define evangelicalism," historian Mark Noll told me, "but nonetheless, it can be approached in such a way as to still say meaningful things about what you want to say meaningful things about."[21] With that wind at my back, I'll say some (hopefully) meaningful things about the object of this defense.

My aim here is to describe more than define, to point toward a center instead of drawing a hard border. Evangelicalism isn't an institution or organization but a movement, a tradition, a manner of worshipping Christ.[22] It's a culture of enthusiasm,[23] a way of life shaped around intimacy with God.[24] It's the maintenance of a deep sense of *personal* responsibility to the truth and to the world. It's the branch of Christianity that never tires of repeating that Jesus died for *you.*[25] As the kids say, it's a vibe.

And as a vibe, evangelicalism has no central office or official creed. There's no pope, no membership roll, no authoritative rubric for who's in and who's out.[26] The reality is that evangelicalism has some fuzzy boundaries.

That doesn't mean *no* boundaries. Evangelicals are necessarily Christians, and usually Christians within a strand of Protestantism that dates to eighteenth-century revivals and twentieth-century organizing. Still, within that bound, the best question is rarely whether someone *is or isn't* evangelical. Instead, we should consider whether someone is *more or less* evangelical.

This strikes me as the better measure on two counts. First, it keeps me from playing "no true evangelical," setting myself up for an easy defense by unilaterally kicking unsavory characters clear out of the movement. I'm not writing *In Defense of Nice Evangelicals Who Think and Vote Exactly as I Do*—or, at least, I don't want to be writing that book. (It should go without saying, but I'm also not commenting on the state of anyone's soul. As ever, there are tares in with the wheat, but it is not for me or you to sort them.)[27]

Second, talking about *more or less* rather than *is or isn't* demands honesty from evangelicalism's critics. Too often missing (or explicitly rejected) in these critiques is a recognition that evangelicalism has a center as well as edges and extremes. Some ideas, practices, and figures are far more typical than others in the median evangelical's experience of our faith.

A useful example is Doug Wilson, the Idaho pastor who willingly embraces the label "theocrat," says the Southern enslaver who "treated his slaves decently" was "a good guy," and uses language like "small-breasted biddies" and "gaytards."[28] Wilson would have to be included in American evangelicalism by any *is or isn't* measure. But if we think instead about *more or less,* Wilson is undeniably *less.*

He believes and emphasizes things that most American evangelicals do not believe and emphasize. He speaks and behaves in ways they generally don't. He writes books they overwhelmingly do not buy and makes podcasts they typically do not download. He has his audience, and he is an evangelical, but as Wilson himself would acknowledge, he's nowhere near *central* to American evangelicalism.[29] He's fringe.

Historian George Marsden famously quipped that "an evangelical is someone who likes Billy Graham."[30] No one would define an evangelical as someone who likes Doug Wilson.

THIS FUZZINESS MAKES talking about evangelicalism—groping around for a sense of who we are and what we're doing here—itself a very evangelical activity.[31] That can include arguing about the term itself. Does it mean what we want it to mean? Do people outside the movement hear politics when we try to talk faith? Has *evangelical* outlived its usefulness?[32]

These debates have run for decades. (In the early 2000s, as soon as Facebook let me write in my own religious affiliation instead of choosing from a drop-down menu, I typed in "Jesus follower" to announce my nineteen-year-old sophistication.) But as with the broader conversation around American evangelicals, the Trump era has intensified things. Some evangelicals, even those who owe their careers to this movement, have toyed with dropping the label.[33]

"The word 'evangelical' now means Trump-voter," biblical scholar Scot McKnight wrote in 2017. "The word 'evangelical' is spoiled."[34]

McKnight is right that *evangelical* is increasingly used in America as a political epithet. That's been true a long time, since the 1970s, and now each exit poll or horse race survey treats "white evangelicals" as a voting bloc.[35] But it's also true that *evangelical* is the best we've got. Messy though the word may be, there's no better alternative available, no term that would be more intelligible or require less explaining.

And for all that debate, a funny thing about evangelicals is that we don't always know we're evangelicals. When I told my mom I'd be writing this book, she listened to my spiel, offered all the requisite congratulations, made me repeat the title three times, and then posed just one question:

"What's an evangelical?"

"Well, *you* are," I said. "We're evangelicals. You're an evangelical."

"I *am?*"

She hadn't the foggiest. And while that's probably rarer now than it was before the internet, even today it's common for longtime evangelicals not to use the term. "I am one of the few people in my church who would regularly use the word *evangelical,*" notes Thomas S. Kidd in his brief history of the movement. "Others, when pressed, might describe themselves as 'Baptist' or 'Bible-believing' or 'born again,'" he continues, but "*evangelical* is a scholarly and journalistic term that doesn't resonate with many laypeople."[36]

This is a real problem given all those polls. When doing more in-depth, religion-focused work, pollsters will drill down to details like denominational affiliation, service attendance rates, and beliefs. But for workaday political polling, the most common method to determine who's an evangelical has just one or two steps.

The first is to ask about self-identification: *Do you consider yourself an evangelical?* Or, perhaps: *Are you an evangelical or born-again Christian?* Something like that, anyway. And since large collections of data don't work well with *more or less,* pollsters use *is or isn't.* If you say *yes,* you're in. *No,* you're out.

Often there's a second step, which is to partially sort respondents by race. Polls tend to have four big categories for Christians in America: Catholics, mainline or non-evangelical Protestants (like Episcopalians), evangelicals, and black Protestants.[37] As I'll discuss more in a moment, black church traditions in America have a great deal in common with their predominantly white evangelical counterparts. But in surveys, if you report being a member of a historically black church, often you'll be excluded from evangelicalism by default.[38]

Of necessity, when I share large-scale data in this book—say, that one in every four or five U.S. adults are evangelicals; that these days we're pretty average by measures like age, income, and education; and that we're increasingly racially diverse[39]—I'll have to rely on research that measures evangelicalism this way. Most surveys use self-ID because it's a quick method any pollster can reproduce, and the results are reasonably reliable. But there are real flaws in self-ID, and they run in both directions: Some people who aren't evangelical tell pollsters they are, while some Christians who fit the bill reject it.[40]

For instance, a 2022 survey found that 10 to 15 percent of American Muslims, Hindus, and people with no religious affiliation self-ID as evangelicals. So do 9 percent of Buddhists, 5 percent of Jews, and 1 percent each of atheists and agnostics. This wasn't a fluke or, as it's sometimes presented, a Trump-era novelty: Multiple surveys dating back to 2012 turn up similar numbers.[41]

These people aren't evangelicals because they aren't Protestant Christians. I know I'm supposed to be doing more description than definition here, but that part is definitional. There's no such thing as an evangelical atheist.[42]

So what's going on here? Well, some of what we're seeing is politics.[43] As McKnight argued, *evangelical* means *Republican* to many, so partly this is people saying they like the GOP.[44] But that pattern didn't hold for all the non-Christian groups. Sometimes, self-ID is just wrong.

The most important case study, though, goes in the other direction. I mentioned that some surveys will ask about two labels, not just one: *evangelical* or *born-again.* When you add *born-again,* a curious thing happens. "When folks talk about evangelicals, it's almost always implied that it's white evangelicals," observes political scientist Ryan Burge, but "the racial group that is the most likely to self-identify as evangelical/born-again is African-Americans. And it's not even close."

In survey data Burge cites from 2022, 45 percent of black Americans self-identify as evangelical or born-again compared to just 25 percent of white respondents.[45] And in another poll from 2021, Pew Research Center found 66 percent of black Protestants in America consider themselves evangelical or born-again compared to only 48 percent of white Protestants.[46]

So then why do we think about evangelicals as mostly white? Well, some of it is because polls isolate historically black churches in that separate category.

But that's not the whole answer. Pollsters unwittingly reinforce the division between black and white Christians in our country, but they didn't create it. Adding *born-again* makes a difference because it's not racially coded like *evangelical* is. Many black Christians are comfortable calling themselves born-again, but only a quarter of black Americans with evangelical beliefs are willing to be called evangelicals.[47]

ONE OF THESE black Christians is Chris Butler, a Chicago minister and political strategist. The evangelical label "feels comfortable to me," he said in an interview, and he doesn't want to "reduce the idea of evangelicalism to racism or even super contemporary political conservatism." That would "give away a legacy in which black folk have invested for a long time." The name recognition and influence that evangelicalism has, Butler added, "We put in on this."

But Butler comes to the word as a pastor. "I spend much of my life in spaces where the theological definition is primary," he noted, and the definition he had in mind was almost certainly the Bebbington quadrilateral.[48]

Introduced by historian David Bebbington in 1989, the Bebbington quadrilateral has been broadly adopted and disputed, borrowed and tweaked. After that baseline recognition that evangelicals are Protestant Christians faithful to core doctrines like the divinity of Christ,[49] the quadrilateral is the standard description of the movement.

"There are the four qualities that have been the special marks of Evangelical religion," Bebbington argued: "conversionism, the belief that lives need to be changed; activism, the expression of the gospel in effort; biblicism, a particular regard for the Bible; and what may be called crucicentrism, a stress on the sacrifice of Christ on the cross."[50] These qualities aren't absent in other parts of the church, but evangelicals give them unique emphasis.

Though often called a theological definition, the quadrilateral is about more than belief, as Bebbington reiterated to me in a call. "I wouldn't want to label my quadrilateral 'theological,'" he said. "It *embraces* theology, but it is a characterization of whatever is important, sociologically *or* theologically. Activism, for example, is not theological, and there are dimensions of conversion that are not theological either, and it is impossible to separate respect for the Bible and its unique standing within the Christian tradition from actually reading it and indeed obeying it."[51] These are matters of both belief and practice, word and deed, ministry and culture, and measured by their fit with the quadrilateral, 18 percent of U.S. adults are evangelicals.[52]

Going to church—and not just going on Sundays but being routinely involved in the life of the local community—is implicit in Bebbington's scheme. But I want to make it explicit too.

"For those who have a deeper understanding of the term's meaning," Kidd contends, "there can be no such thing as a nonchurchgoing evangelical."[53] In the spirit of *more or less,* I won't go quite that far. But outside of exceptional circumstances like chronic illness or disability, routine churchgoing is essential.[54] Usually, if you aren't in church, your evangelicalism is very much *less.*[55]

Centering a description like the quadrilateral helps us remember that evangelicalism is more than predominantly white American churches—and much more than votes for Trump. This movement well pre-dated that usage and well exceeds it around the world today.[56]

Nearly nine in ten evangelicals live outside of North America, mostly in Asia and sub-Saharan Africa;[57] and in the United States, Latinos are the fastest-growing evangelical demographic.[58] The quadrilateral also loops in many Christians in the Pentecostal and charismatic traditions. Not the churches all-in on the prosperity gospel, which is a very different emphasis, but certainly many congregations that prize the giftings of the Spirit.[59]

Moreover, while I understand—and will discuss at length in chapter 3—the grim U.S. history that separated the historic black church and white evangelicals on Sunday mornings, it seems undeniable to me that we are far more alike than different by the quadrilateral's measure.[60] Something like first cousins, perhaps, or siblings half-estranged.

Bebbington agrees. "I'm convinced of the equal evangelicalism of the black church," he told me, while recognizing that often "they're not used to using the term, and they're very skeptical of the term precisely because of the association with which it's been loaded" across three centuries.[61]

WE'LL TALK MORE history later, so for now just a few words on those centuries will suffice. The story of evangelicalism begins with the First Great Awakening, that huge revival led by lively preachers like John Wesley and George Whitefield. It swept through the United Kingdom and the American colonies in the decades leading up to the Revolution.

Evangelical was first employed as a noun in 1807,[62] but that use wasn't widely adopted until the 1970s.[63] Early on, revived and newly converted Christians talked about becoming serious, being "awakened" to "true religion."[64] For 150 years or so, there was comparatively little distinction between evangelicals and other Protestants, but around the turn of the twentieth century, American Protestantism split.

On one side were modernists, or liberals, Christians who were coming to treat the Bible as less authoritative. They were focused more on social action than the supernatural, questioning or even discarding doctrines like the virgin birth of Jesus and his bodily resurrection. On the other side were fundamentalists, theologically conservative Christians who embraced those "fundamentals" of the faith.[65]

The fundamentalist-modernist conflict came to a head in Dayton, Tennessee, in 1925 with a case, often called the Scopes Monkey Trial, about teaching evolution in public schools. In court, the fundamentalists won. But they lost public favor, and after that, the split was complete.[66] The modernists became what we now call mainline Protestants, while the fundamentalists substantially retreated from public life.

"Out of mainstream sight [fundamentalists] were expected to be out of mind of the larger public," historian Martin E. Marty recounts:

> Of course, most Americans were aware that in the back country there were hillbillies, rednecks, holy rollers, tent revivalists, Bible colleges, and evangelistic radio stations and publishing companies. But these were segregated in the Bible Belts of the Midwest and especially the South. They did not count for much, especially since their vision of the public

> order usually seemed negative. They disapproved of worldliness or immorality, but one seldom saw them approaching the halls of secular power to make their case. They were not much at home in the higher academy. Since they were out of step with modernity, they were expected increasingly to disappear.[67]

But they didn't disappear. And in the late 1940s and early 1950s, a subset of more educated fundamentalists decided they didn't want to be in the backcountry anymore.

Fundamentalism had become "the modern priest and Levite, bypassing suffering humanity," charged Carl F. H. Henry, who would become the first editor of *Christianity Today*. "The picture is clear when one brings into focus such admitted social evils as aggressive warfare, racial hatred and intolerance, the liquor traffic, and exploitation of labor or management, whichever it may be. The social reform movements dedicated to the elimination of such evils do not have the active, let alone vigorous, cooperation of large segments of evangelical Christianity."[68]

The time had come, Henry and other new evangelicals decided, to rejoin public life and work for its betterment. The movement would find a champion in Billy Graham, whose revivals attracted millions the world over and who cooperated with Catholic and mainline Christians in a way fundamentalists would not.[69]

Come 1976, *evangelical* entered common parlance in America. The election of Jimmy Carter, a born-again Southern Baptist, was a landmark moment—but so was the rise of the religious right, which spurred white evangelical voters to help cast Carter out of the White House in 1980.[70]

MANY HISTORIES STOP here or else leap straight ahead to 2016, treating the 1980s and 1990s evangelicalism of politicos like Ronald Reagan and Ralph Reed and pastor-pundits like Pat Robertson and Tim LaHaye as the movement's final form. Contemporary evangelicalism is presented as a powerful, politicized brute whose true nature was laid bare by Donald Trump. This narrative is mistaken.

Yes, there is a real consistency across not just decades but centuries. As historian Molly Worthen has observed, the Bebbington quadrilateral lists "a set of qualities that we can find in [progressive evangelical] Jim Wallis or [religious right leader] Jerry Falwell, in the eighteenth century or the twenty-first."[71]

But there are real changes too. For better and worse, the movement isn't static. For instance, from the Scopes trial of 1925 up through the early 2000s, evolution remained a major point of contention for evangelicals. But today, two-thirds of evangelicals believe God used evolution to create humanity, and only a quarter still say we've existed in our "present form since the beginning of time."[72] That's an enormous shift, and it's only one of many recent changes in how we live, think, and worship.[73]

And it's not only evangelicals who've changed. When Billy Graham went to Manhattan in 1957, he packed Madison Square Garden for sixteen weeks. ABC News aired hours of his revivals on national TV. *The New York Times* printed his sermons. The crowds outgrew the Garden's capacity, so Graham filled Yankee Stadium with one hundred thousand people.[74]

We don't live in that world anymore. It was only a year before the Manhattan revivals that *Christianity Today*—which Graham helped found—had described evangelicalism as "neglected, slighted, misrepresented." All was not rosy then, but in some ways, evangelicalism was on the upswing. For all of that society's evils, Christianity was more the cultural default. Public religiosity was subject to critique but also broadly normal. That is true no more.

Now, it's important not to overstate the change. Evangelicals in America have a reputation for our persecution complex, our inclination to exaggerate accounts of our own suffering and treat mere opposition as oppression.[75]

That reputation isn't wrong, and American evangelicals are not persecuted, full stop.

Sometimes we do have to sacrifice for our faith, but we aren't subjected to the kind of abuse Christians have suffered in other times and places. The United States remains a unique bastion of freedom of religion, speech, and assembly.

Even culturally and legally similar countries can't compare. In England, the police can and will arrest you for rude tweets.[76] In Finland in 2022, a lawmaker and a pastor were tried (and, thankfully, acquitted) for quoting New Testament passages about homosexuality.[77] Whatever our troubles in America—including appalling encroachments on due process and privacy rights—we don't do that here. Our government violates the Bill of Rights, but at least we *have* a Bill of Rights. And contrary to what some evangelicals suggest, public disparagement, even from powerful people, isn't persecution.[78]

STILL, DISPARAGEMENT ISN'T nothing. Nor are misunderstanding, cynicism, or disdain.

In 2015, drawing on national survey data, sociologists George Yancey and David A. Williamson found significant hostility toward conservative Christians in America, particularly among people with "a relatively high degree of social power in our society."[79]

Survey respondents joked that they'd like to see Christians martyred as they were in the Roman Empire: "So many Christians, so few lions," two separate participants said. "I wish we could start feeding them to the lions again," snarked another, "or burn them at the stake." Still others talked about hitting Christians with terrorist attacks, eugenics, exile, forced lobotomies, or "[eradication] without hesitation or remorse."[80]

As Yancey and Williamson are quick to note, these are indeed jokes. They're not real threats. But they do reveal a real animosity—and a certain social comfort. The people who laughed about lions and lobotomies didn't think they were saying something beyond the pale—and, in their circles, they probably weren't.[81] That's true in many American contexts a decade later as well; an enormously popular progressive podcast, for instance, decries evangelical faith as "white trash, magical thinking, dumb people bullshit" and routinely calls evangelicals "cancer" and the "worst people" in our country.[82] More recent survey research has likewise turned up similar (if less vivid) results. A 2023 Pew poll, for example, found evangelicals were more likely to be viewed negatively by fellow Americans than any other major religious group.[83]

It may be partially our own fault that evangelicals are unpopular. Many people would argue exactly that, and I'll consider the case against us in the pages to come. And regardless of cause, *persecution* is too strong a word for what we experience.

Yet unfair censure does not have to rise to the level of persecution to warrant a response, and this pattern of censure is unfair.

As my former *Christianity Today* colleague Daniel Silliman mused when I talked to him about this book, I think it is possible to acknowledge evangelicalism's faults and failures and "still think evangelicalism is worthwhile and good. I think it is possible to say, *Yep, all that stuff is wrong—and also, that is not the sum total of evangelicalism.*"[84]

I think it's possible to be honest about evangelicalism and still conclude it's overdue for a good defense.

IN DEFENSE OF EVANGELICALISM

CHAPTER ONE

INSINCERITY

If you look at how they behave, it's clear evangelicals are actually about cultural and political identity, not belief.

"I BELIEVE IN Jesus Christ, the Son of God, sent from God to die in my place," Rogerio told me. "And that's what I believe."

We were sitting in an airy lobby of the urban Pittsburgh megachurch that hosts the immigrant advocacy center where he works. Outside, a colorful, two-story mural declared the multiethnic congregation's commitment to "following Jesus in a diverse community." Inside, we were talking across a café table positioned behind the requisite coffee shop and next to the indoor playground, complete with climbing wall. Children trooped up the stairs for an after-school program, and the receptionist kept busy buzzing people in. I'd asked Rogerio, himself an immigrant from Brazil, what he meant when he called himself an evangelical, and he'd answered without hesitation. But he wasn't done yet.

"I believe in the Bible as the authoritative Word of God, and I do—or try to do my best to—follow and obey its commands," he continued. "My faith is personal, and I have my beliefs in what the Bible says and what the Holy Spirit guides me to do." He nodded toward his denomination's doctrinal standards, then pivoted from faith to deeds.

"One thing that I like about what I do is that we decided from the beginning not to get involved in the politics," Rogerio said of his advocacy work. "And I believe that this should be what we as Christians do as well. The politics divided us, but as Christians we have one mandate: to assist our neighbors, to love them. Jesus came and said, *You need to love them as you love yourself.* So that's what I live for."[1]

ROGERIO'S ACCOUNT OF his beliefs was fervent, earnest, the embodiment of 1 Peter 3:15, in which the apostle enjoins us to "be prepared to give an answer to everyone who asks you to give the reason for the hope that you have," and to do so "with gentleness and respect."[2]

It was also entirely unremarkable. This is how evangelicals talk. It's how evangelicals think. "If any one mark clearly identifies them it is their total belief in an awesome, supernatural Jesus Christ," *Time* magazine wrote of young evangelical converts in 1971. And "not just a marvelous man who lived 2,000 years ago but a living God who is both Savior and Judge, the ruler of their destinies. Their lives revolve around the necessity for an intense personal relationship with that Jesus, and the belief that such a relationship should condition every human life."[3]

Rogerio may be uncommonly well spoken, his answer polished by seminary education and readied by years of presentations of his faith to the immigrants he serves. Even so, what he said is typical. It's the kind of thing millions of evangelicals would say.

"Among all the major Christian traditions in the contemporary United States, evangelicalism exhibits the highest degree of adherence to many of the traditionally orthodox Christian theological beliefs," sociologist Christian Smith explains in *American Evangelicalism: Embattled and Thriving*, a milestone study of the movement published in 1998. And that adherence is more than memorization, more than the capacity to rattle off answers for a pollster.

In addition to a national survey, Smith and his research team conducted hundreds of detailed interviews with churchgoing Protestants. Those conversations "substantiate[d] our survey data on beliefs, confirming that those who identify as evangelicals manifest very high degrees of concern with adherence" to orthodoxy, Smith writes. "Most evangelicals we interviewed pointed to right beliefs about God, the Bible, and salvation as central to their religious identities and values."[4]

The interview snippets Smith shares range across evangelical church traditions, yet they all sound just like Rogerio. "I believe that the whole Bible is true," said one Reformed woman. "I believe that Jesus Christ is the Son of God, and that he came into the world to save us, and he died on the cross and rose again from the dead, and he is sitting at our Father's right hand."[5]

A woman in the Christian and Missionary Alliance denomination struck very similar notes. "Evangelicals believe that the Bible is the inspired Word of God and the whole truth," she told Smith's team. "Our first tenet is preaching Jesus Christ as the Gospel."[6]

Smith's study went beyond theology to activism, practice, and politics, and there too he found that characteristic enthusiasm and care. "If ever liberal Protestantism was distinguished by its social-Gospel activism, it appears to be so no more," he writes. "The evidence suggests, instead, that evangelicals may be the most committed carriers of a new social Gospel."[7]

This evidence was consistent in the national numbers and in-depth conversations alike. Smith's interviewees vocally rejected a "compartmentalized 'Sunday-morning' faith," a Christianity that moves the head but not the hands. As a Presbyterian man put it, "We're called to love our neighbor. That's society. So [we need to be concerned about] anything going on out there [that] affects your neighbor. And we need to love them. So social issues, like hunger or poverty, economic issues, social issues like divorce, crime, abortion, however people are hurting."[8]

Other interviewees were just as effusive. "Not having faith would totally reorder my whole life. Even my thought life would be different," said one woman. If she doesn't care for people in need, "I have to question whether I really believe" in Jesus, said another. Evangelical faith is "costly on a daily basis," explained a third. "You know? Costly to love. Because it always throws my heart out there, instead of just living for myself. It's costly to serve other people. So I would say it's really reoriented my life."[9]

It would come as a surprise to these folks to learn that none of this is real—that all their beliefs and purpose and service and sacrifice are, at best, a well-intended self-delusion or, more likely, a self-serving and politicized tribalism. It would come as such a surprise as to be literally incredible to them.

Yet this is a common charge against American evangelicals. "Increasingly, those who identify as evangelical are aligning not primarily with a theological system but with a cultural and political identity," wrote *Jesus and John Wayne* author Kristin Kobes Du Mez in 2021.[10]

Evangelicalism "has become about shared political convictions," argued *Washington Post* columnist Shadi Hamid in 2024, with self-ID motivated by "what it [means] politically, most of all [as] a way to signal support for Donald Trump."[11]

"In the main," contended former evangelical Peter Wehner at *The Atlantic* the same year, "the white evangelical movement has for decades exacerbated our divisions, fueled hatreds and grievances, and turned fellow citizens into enemies rather than friends. This isn't true of all evangelicals," he allowed. "But it is fair to say that this movement that was at one time defined by its theological commitments is now largely defined by its partisan ones."[12]

Now, there is *a* truth here. Remember the Muslim and Buddhist "evangelicals" from the introduction? That self-ID is wrong, but it does exist, and it's not meaningless. It tells us something that these people who reject the evangelical tradition still want the label. Consciously or not, they've realized that *evangelical* has taken on political meaning in America. They've concluded—incorrectly but not unreasonably—that "to be very religiously engaged and very politically conservative means that they are evangelical," as Ryan Burge, the political scientist, has explained at *The New York Times*.[13]

So Du Mez, Hamid, Wehner, and critics like them might argue that Rogerio and other evangelicals who understand their faith as he does are the outliers. Holdovers, maybe. Anachronisms who'd be more at home in the evangelicalism of the 1990s, when Smith published *Embattled and Thriving*. They're the exceptions Wehner grants, those "good and gracious people who seek to be peacemakers, including in the political realm."[14]

That kind of caveat is a good start and evidence of an effort at good-faith engagement.

But these allegations of evangelical insincerity turn on two errors. One is the mistaken acceptance of a simplistic, self-ID version of evangelicalism—an *is or isn't* model in which anyone who declares themselves evangelical simply *is,* no matter how short they fall by every other measure. Hamid describes "evangelicals" who don't go to church, don't believe in the divinity of Christ, and, in some cases, affirm different religions entirely.

Their self-ID tells us a lot about contemporary politics. It tells us a lot about how the media uses *evangelical* these days. But it tells us nearly nothing about evangelicalism itself. This is a movement with some fuzzy boundaries, but it's not an empty container into which anyone can pour anything and everything. If atheists call themselves evangelicals because they like Trump, that doesn't mean evangelicalism includes atheism. It means those atheists are low-information voters who've been grossly misinformed.

Imagine having this conversation about other major religions or branches of the church. For the sake of argument, let's say that the black church in America should be excluded from evangelicalism and treated as a separate movement. This is a revealing comparison because the "very high level of evangelical support for Donald Trump is like nothing seen in America's recent religious-political history," observes Mark Noll, the historian, "except for the even higher percentage that since the 1960s Democrats have received from Bible-believing, born-again African Americans."[15]

Now suppose polls began to show that some subset of people with no connection to the historic black church were beginning to self-identify into it to signal their affinity for the Democratic Party. Suppose we had atheists, nones, and Hindus telling pollsters they consider themselves part of the black church.

Have these people joined the local Church of God in Christ congregation? They have not. Do they worship with the National Baptist Convention? Nope. Do they believe any basic Christian doctrines or orient their lives around the distinctive spiritual practices of the black church? Not a one! So would it be reasonable, on the basis of these polls, to conclude that the black church tradition is a "movement that was at one time defined by its theological commitments" but "is now largely defined by its partisan ones"?

It would not. It would be laughable, ridiculous, insulting. We would not accept that self-ID. We would reject it, and rightly so. We would recognize that this tradition, though not a unified institution, has a center, a history, a substance. We would respect the self-understanding of those who are *more* typical of its commitments and character. We wouldn't declare *black church* irretrievably stained by politics because ignorant voters are politicizing the term.

Evangelicalism deserves that same courtesy. It's fair to say that some people who call themselves evangelicals are aligning with a political identity, signaling support for Trump, and turning fellow citizens into enemies. It's also fair to say that evangelicals are most often discussed in the press in connection to our politics and, not coincidentally, increasingly understood as a political bloc by our non-evangelical neighbors.

But it's not fair to say that evangelicalism is "primarily" about politics rather than faith, that the movement as a whole is "about shared political convictions," that "in the main" evangelicalism "fuel[s] hatreds and grievances." That is not true.

To see the second error, it's instructive to look at Wehner's reasons for dropping the evangelical label himself. As he wrote in 2017, he once saw evangelicalism as an "imperfect forc[e] for good," an "effort to faithfully represent Christ in word and deed" with an admirable record of activism in abolitionism, the pro-life movement, and more. This is all very apt, very familiar, very Bebbington.

In the Trump era, however, Wehner said he's come to believe evangelicalism is irreparably tainted. Favorably quoting an unnamed ministry leader, he pronounced the word *evangelical* "now a tribal rather than a creedal description." It's "not a religious identification so much as a political one"—and one Wehner rejected.[16]

I want to be careful to avoid suggesting that Wehner was rejecting more than he intended to reject. He wrote this article in a moment of high scandal, when a Republican Senate candidate stood accused of sexual misconduct and assault by nine women, one of whom was just fourteen at the time of the alleged encounter. The candidate would go on to lose, but exit polling indicated that white self-identified evangelical voters backed him at the same rate (around 80 percent) that they've gone for Republicans in most races over the past fifty years.[17] This is just what Wehner anticipated and mourned.

Moreover, we should notice that nothing in the essay suggests Wehner changed his own faith. Not his beliefs, not his church, none of it. By every measure but self-ID, he was just as evangelical as before.

So if the first error is accepting the self-identification of those who are demonstrably *not* evangelical, the second error is discounting the self-understanding of those who *are* evangelical, and particularly those whose evangelicalism is typical of the movement—those nearer the center than the edge.

And when you ask those people what it means for them to be evangelical, they don't answer in the political terms Wehner describes and denounces.

They don't talk about Donald Trump if you ask for the meaning of their evangelicalism. They talk about Jesus.

Wehner has come to see evangelicalism as a partisan tribe, but *they* haven't.

THE VERSION OF the insincerity allegation from Wehner, Hamid, and Du Mez includes another important caveat: time. In this telling, evangelicalism's devolution into a right-wing political tribe is a recent phenomenon. It wasn't always this way. And though the conclusion is overstated, this premise is correct. Evangelicals have long been subject to disdain, but in the past, it was more religious in focus. We were "Bible thumpers" and "Jesus freaks," even to many in the GOP.

A more sweeping version of the insincerity claim dispenses with that timeline, arguing that evangelicalism was *always* organized around identity, not belief.

In the more evenhanded and academic version of the charge, the identity is more cultural than political, and evangelicalism isn't unique. All religion, on this view, is about tribe, not doctrine. In the angrier, popular-level version, evangelicalism is uniquely insincere, and its identity is squarely and maliciously political—about power and its acquisition, about stomping on the face of everyone who isn't a white Republican.

A succinct example of the academic version comes from a sociologist named Samuel L. Perry. Best known for his influential research on Christian nationalism (to which I'll turn in chapter 5), Perry is also the author of *Religion for Realists: Why We*

All Need the Scientific Study of Religion. Much of the book is addressed to fellow sociologists, and Perry ably argues that academia must recover from its blind spot on religion to understand the world accurately.

But Perry's own understanding of faith is strangely *un*realistic. It's one thing to say beliefs are one factor of many in religious people's lives, jostling around in our brains with less conscious influences like culture and politics, family and personality, ignorance and knowledge. But Perry goes much further. Identity is what matters, he says, and beliefs are objectively irrelevant.

He states this plainly and repeatedly, inviting readers to "start thinking more in terms of unconscious bias and group loyalties than self-conscious beliefs; more about fertility rates, cohorts, and immigration than doctrines."[18]

You may have qualms about that framework, but Perry advises you to put your qualms aside. Think about beliefs narrowly, as disembodied doctrines of the afterlife and evangelism, not communal norms, values, or responsibilities. If you thought faith "motivates human beings," he writes, or that ideas and dogmas shape "religious communities and broader societies," or that individuals can and must make meaningful decisions in our lives, then you thought wrong—"empirically wrong," in fact.[19]

Belief is not "really the driver of religious activity," Perry says, nor "what makes people 'religious' or 'irreligious.'" Indeed, "religion isn't fundamentally about faith, or even the content of one's faith. At the level of cognitive and emotional processes, it's about our relationships to in-group and out-group members. Religion is sacralized 'us-ness.'"[20]

Our lives, then, are oriented not around God or Scripture or even the church as the body of Christ. It's simple tribalism,

Perry contends. Group identity is the truth of religion, and all the theology and practice we layer on top amounts to after-the-fact justifications and storytelling to shore up our status and justify excluding other people.[21]

A LESS SWEEPING version of this argument could've been insightful and persuasive.[22] Any reasonable adult knows people have multiple and complicated motives for how we live. Our options are limited, our choices constrained. We're influenced by our friends and those we admire. We mistake our tastes for ethics and our instincts for facts. We don't reliably know our own minds. We don't consistently live in the faith we profess. We are tired and unwitting and weak.

"I do not understand what I do," exclaimed the apostle Paul. "For I have the desire to do what is good, but I cannot carry it out. For I do not do the good I want to do, but the evil I do not want to do—this I keep on doing."[23] Rogerio told me he believes in the Bible as the authoritative Word of God and obeys its commands, but then he caught himself: I "try to do my best" to obey it, he said.

Perry suggests that if we make the "fundamental error [of] assuming theological beliefs determine our religious behaviors," we'll "find ourselves puzzled and frustrated that religious beliefs and behaviors often don't line up as we would expect them to." He gives the example of "Christians who proclaim a gospel of universal love while worshipping in racially segregated churches."[24]

But I can't say I'm particularly puzzled. Scripture and experience alike say we aren't creatures of pure belief. Doctrine is not automation. Sanctification is not immediate. *The evil I do not want to do—this I keep on doing.*

If anything, I'd be surprised if social science found that religious beliefs and behaviors *did* line up perfectly in most believers. The rarity of saints does not prove Perry's claim that "our theological 'beliefs' (e.g., those creeds we recite on Sunday mornings or fight about on social media) are often more like a junk drawer of sayings" to signal group identity.[25] It proves the Christian doctrine of sin—which is, incidentally, in the creeds.

PERRY PROVIDES A clear distillation of the case for reducing faith to tribe. But it's a weak case, confused and unable to account for why religious groups think and behave as they do.[26]

That lack is striking in Perry's discussion of American evangelicals. For instance, citing national survey data, he finds that conservative Protestants who watch a lot of pornography in their teenage years are more likely than others to have doubts about their faith in their young adulthood.

What explains that? Perry says that while other people will simply "live with the incongruence," it bothers conservative Christians, so they try to "resolve that contradiction either by changing their sexual behavior (often more easily said than done) or changing their theological beliefs."[27]

Religion for Realists presents this as an example of disconnect between belief and behavior, but surely it's just the opposite: These young Christians try to quit porn or else deconstruct or deconvert because their beliefs *do* matter to them greatly. Even in leaving the faith, they're taking it seriously, allowing it to shape their lives. If group identity were everything, why bother? For such a common and besetting sin, conservative Christians could simply adjust the in-group story to accommodate porn use, keeping morale and membership numbers high. Only if doctrine matters does this pattern make sense.

Similarly, Perry reports that evangelicals and other conservative Christians score lower than average on tests about scientific knowledge. But the difference disappears if you take out questions on topics, like evolution, where theology comes into play. This suggests religious conservatives "simply reject scientific claims that violate teachings at the core of their Christian identity," Perry comments.[28]

Perhaps. Or, if we want a more plausible and less convoluted explanation, it suggests that they reject claims that they *believe to be false.* That's undoubtedly what they'd say if asked. They're not stupid or tribal, just trying to be faithful.

One last example. In contrast to Western Protestants, Perry notes, people in other faiths elsewhere in the world "seem to understand their religion as primarily about community tradition, embodied practices, shared readings, special clothing, holy objects, sacred spaces, and most importantly, who they are to the world, not whether they believe certain doctrines from which their whole lives must logically proceed."[29]

They get it, you see: They know all this religion stuff is really about marking social territory, celebrating holidays, and keeping the kids in line.

But Perry also recounts a trip to Florida he took with a Christian youth organization in the summer between high school and college. Down in Daytona in 1998, he writes, the students' "social times were spent ritually performing every purity culture cliché: side hugs, girls in one-piece bathing suits, guys swimming in T-shirts, group dates, guarding hearts, confessing lust daily, all of it."[30]

There's plenty to dislike about the gracelessness of 1990s purity culture, and plenty here that warrants at least a gentle snicker. I myself spent far too much of middle school swimming in a skirted leotard I was beginning to outgrow, convinced I'd never find another suit of adequate modesty. But why is it wisdom if people in other faiths prioritize "special clothes," yet it's somehow worthy of derision when evangelicals believe our clothing choices actually mean something to God? What's wrong with wanting your whole life to logically proceed from your best understanding of the truth? Is that bad?

Sometimes evangelicals are cringe, I know. We do have a culture, and it does tend to be corny and heavy handed. Our art can be derivative, our music sentimental. All that is true. But whatever else we are, evangelicals are sincere about our faith. Evangelicalism *is* about belief in Jesus Christ, the Son of God.

WHILE PERRY IS scholarly and dispassionate, John Pavlovitz writes in a mood of perpetual outrage. An author and former pastor, his Substack following is north of one hundred thousand,[31] and his account routinely ranks in the top five of the newsletter platform's bestsellers in the Faith & Spirituality category.[32] That means thousands of people pay him at least a few bucks a month to read his work. Though Pavlovitz mostly writes outside traditional publishing and media, his Substack newsletter is influential. An indulgent mix of fury and condescension, threats of ostracism and visions of comeuppance, it's very popular.

While much of what he writes would fit in chapter 2—he

routinely describes evangelicals and our beliefs as hateful, racist, sexist, and rejected by Christ himself—Pavlovitz also alleges that belief is not really the organizing principle of evangelicalism, and he reserves this critique for white American evangelicals alone.[33]

The white evangelical church "has failed Jesus," Pavlovitz writes. "They have misappropriated his likeness, hijacked his name, and weaponized his [message] into something grotesque and oppressive," something that serves only "the tiny gated community of the white and the wealthy." That is, something that serves the in-group.[34]

(In reality, American evangelicals are not especially wealthy. Per Pew self-ID data, our income is now about average, but just two decades ago, we were disproportionately low-income.)[35]

Why this hijacking? Politics, of course. Getting more power.[36] Evangelicals are venomous, Pavlovitz says, part of a "white Republican theocracy built on power, exclusion, and subjugation," telling themselves stories "to validate and justify the harm they do to so many people."[37] The ones who voted for Trump "created and embraced a bastardized, frankensteined religion made of power, greed, white supremacy, and intolerance of difference."[38] They love the Bible, sure, but only because "it makes a great hammer with which you can beat the hell out of your neighbor." They love God, but only the god of their tribe.[39]

In an open letter addressed "to hateful white Americans," Pavlovitz wishes they could feel "compassion for the humanity around you: not just those you love, not just those who look, sound, worship, vote, and think like you. I wish you could find empathy beyond those you believe are your people: your family, your tribe, your party, your country."[40] The letter's discussion of God and Trump (not to mention Pavlovitz's whole shtick) suggests the hateful white Americans in question are evangelicals.

THIS IS ALL very energetic. But is it *true*? I don't think so. Certainly not this comprehensive denunciation. To hear Pavlovitz tell it, you'd think every evangelical church was a franchise of Westboro Baptist, the family cult in Kansas known for showing up at military funerals with signs reading "God hates fags." That's not reality. That's not what evangelicals are like.

To state the obvious: Hate, greed, and white supremacy are grotesquely destructive sins, and they are sins that—along with many more—are undeniably found in American evangelicalism. I don't want to downplay or dismiss it. American evangelicals are sinners! And white evangelicals' record on race is the single most difficult part of our history, including quite recent history.

I know this firsthand. The Christian school where I went to kindergarten was founded in the 1970s as a segregation academy, a private school designed to exclude black children while public education desegregated. That kind of history is uncomfortably close, disturbingly common, and categorically wrong.[41]

But it isn't the whole of the evangelical story. That school was quite literally founded on hate—but today it's a very different institution. It has not only desegregated but also publicly confessed and repented of its racist past. Confession doesn't undo that past. Nothing can. Still, it's a meaningful change and as much a part of evangelicalism as the school's segregated founding. To deny the white supremacy at that founding would be a lie. And to ignore the school's repentance and reformation would be a lie too.

I'll return to matters of race in greater detail later. For now, the point is that Pavlovitz-style accusations of tribal malice are risibly distorted. The notion that this tradition doesn't take belief seriously is ludicrous. Talking to many evangelicals is like playing Six Degrees of Kevin Bacon, only instead of Kevin Bacon, it's Jesus, and you pretty much never need all six degrees.

YOU CAN EVEN see the centrality and sincerity of belief in our buying habits. Each year, the Evangelical Christian Publishers Association puts out lists of top-selling books, those that reach milestones of one hundred thousand, five hundred thousand, one million, and ten million sales or more. And each year, the books bought most are . . . Bibles. And Bible studies. And books about the Bible. And devotionals, and guidance on prayer and other spiritual disciplines, and theological works ranging from systematic tomes to accessible explanations of Christ's humility and love.[42]

These evangelical publishers put out plenty of other books. They have more strident offerings, more political offerings, plenty of fiction. Those are overwhelmingly not the top sellers. Evangelicals say our faith is about belief in Christ and fidelity to the Bible, and we spend and read like that's true.

This isn't to say every evangelical can perfectly articulate the doctrine of the Trinity or that evangelicalism is never swayed by cultural or political winds. Smith found that evangelicals are unusually interested in right doctrine, but we're hardly immune to error.

A few times each decade, two evangelical organizations, Ligonier Ministries and Lifeway Research, partner to examine the beliefs of Americans who affirm the Bebbington quadrilateral (those emphases of conversion, activism, Bible, and cross). In 2025, the researchers found that many American evangelicals revealed "an alarming lack of biblical literacy, as well as a tendency to hold contradictory beliefs without seeming to recognize the incongruity."[43]

This study shows many evangelicals "are confused about the nature of God and his relationship with the world he has created," Glenn R. Kreider, a theology professor at Dallas Theological Seminary, told *Christianity Today*. "It also demonstrates inconsistency in beliefs, even to the point of contradiction."[44]

As an evangelical, I find this all quite troubling (though I'd note that some of the results look rather less grim if you don't subscribe to a Reformed tradition, like Presbyterianism, which is linked to the Reformer John Calvin and is only one version of evangelical belief). Yet I also recognize that the mere fact of this survey—the fact that Ligonier and Lifeway put resources toward this project, that Kreider expressed his disappointment, that *Christianity Today* reported the story, that I and thousands of other American evangelicals are reading it and shaking our heads and sending it out in the group chat with exasperated commentary—is *very evangelical.*

We are troubled because belief *does* matter to us. We are self-policing because we sincerely care about getting this stuff right. Evangelicals are sinners, but evangelicalism is not just sin all the way down. The skepticism or outright suspicion underlying the insincerity charge from Pavlovitz, Perry, and others isn't warranted. It doesn't hold up under scrutiny. It doesn't survive contact with ordinary evangelicals like Rogerio.

JUST A FEW miles up the road from Rogerio's church, I met Taylor in the corner of a local coffee shop. Taylor is about thirty, thoughtful, and so soft-spoken that I worried my recorder wouldn't catch what he was saying. He grew up in evangelicalism, went to an evangelical college, and is raising his own kids in an evangelical church today.

We got together to talk about how he voted for president in 2024 and the belief-driven way he made that choice. "I was raised to believe voting was important, and I think voting is important for me now," Taylor told me. He backed Mitt Romney in 2012, then found himself in a quandary in 2016. "I was like, *I cannot vote for either of these people,*" he said of Hillary Clinton and Donald Trump, and he didn't. In 2020, he went for Joe Biden, hoping that a change in administrations might end the COVID-19 pandemic more quickly.

After that, Taylor recalled, he "thought we were never going to have to deal with this again. Trump had lost. Biden had said he wasn't going to run again. But then I wake up in 2024, and it feels like it's 2020." As the party nominations were made and Election Day neared, he was in turmoil.

On the one hand, "who Trump portrays himself to be—whether or not it's accurate—is not something that I agree with. For me, I really struggle with that as a Christian," Taylor said. Beyond personal character, Taylor also worried that Trump's belligerence toward other countries would draw the United States into a major new war.

But without the pandemic affecting his calculations, Taylor found the Democratic ticket's agenda unacceptable. "On the other side, everything that Kamala Harris stood for and believed in, I didn't stand for," he explained. "This is what was happening in my head: *Do I want peace at the cost of LGBTQ insanity, or do I want economic health at the cost of peace?* That was the decision I felt like I was making."

Taylor spent *months* weighing this choice. He went back and forth, turning things over in his mind, deciding on one candidate, then the other, then back again. He considered refusing to vote, as he had in 2016, but he felt a responsibility to do the best he could with the viable options available.

Ultimately, after "much agonizing," he voted for Trump—and a year later, his agonizing continued. "I still feel terrible about it," Taylor said, launching into another round of gaming out the costs and benefits of either election outcome.[45]

If I had a magic machine to make the opposite of the cruel, unthinking, authoritarian evangelicals Pavlovitz imagines, I'd make someone a lot like Taylor. As it happens, I don't need a machine, because Taylor already exists. His voting record is more varied and his internal debate more conflicted than that of most people, evangelical or not. But I don't think he's unusual among evangelicals in his care about his faith and its implications for his life.

Toward the end of his first letter to the Corinthian church, the apostle Paul takes up the theme of resurrection and its import. If "Christ has not been raised, our preaching is useless and so is your faith," he writes. If Jesus did not rise from the dead, he did not rescue us from sin and death. Our faith is worthless, and Christians who have died are gone forever. "If only for this life we have hope in Christ, we are of all people most to be pitied," Paul recognizes. "And as for us [evangelists], why do we endanger ourselves every hour?" It makes sense only if Jesus is alive.[46]

Something similar might be said of evangelicals. Political

tribalism and cultural identity aren't enough to explain why we do what we do.

It's impossible to go to an evangelical church on a Sunday morning and come away honestly convinced that faith is irrelevant there, that the whole thing is a self-serving charade, that these people are having prayer meetings and studying the Bible and organizing meal trains and serving at homeless shelters and giving altar calls as some sort of elaborate disguise of hidden, power-mad intentions. That's absurd. Evangelicalism makes sense only if folks really believe it—and for all our flaws, we do.

CHAPTER TWO

EVIL

Okay, I'll concede that evangelicalism really is about belief. But the beliefs are harmful and bad.

MATTHEW MILLINER WAS getting animated. "I know there are abusive elements in evangelicalism," he said. "I know there are awful realities. I don't think people are making that up. But not all of us have experienced that, and we're not retraumatizing someone if we say, *Wow, I have seen long-term, unflashy fidelity,*" if we recognize that "there is something to be said for this movement that activated—praise be to God!—my own faith."

Milliner is an art history professor at Chicago's Wheaton College, a well-connected institution sometimes dubbed the "evangelical Harvard." I'd reached out for a conversation after reading an article of his on "growing disillusioned with disillusion."

There's "nothing wrong with honest critique" of evangelicalism, Milliner had written, but he'd become exasperated with rebukes that, particularly in aggregate, looked not so much prophetic as profitable. In some circles, he said, it "almost seem[s] that the normative way to advance your career [is] to be the first to undermine what [is] left of the evangelical movement. Indeed, this continues to be one very effective way to build a podcast audience or a speaking platform."[1]

As we spoke, though, it was clear that the primary source of Milliner's animation was not his frustration with cynical critique but his affection and gratitude for evangelicalism's uncelebrated goods.

"God is faithful," he told me, "and it's just not written about. It's not talked about because the algorithms reward the negative, and we are living in an algorithmically driven age. All these bad things are true—but the *majority* report is about people like my youth pastor [who helped bring me to faith], and he's just preaching grace. I could tell story after story after story of that."[2]

So could I. But the question of this chapter is whether such stories are an illusion—whether the reality, as some critics allege, is that evangelicalism is a system of bad beliefs that bear bad fruit.

WHEN EIGHT IN ten white evangelical votes went to Donald Trump in 2016, questions abounded. How could the people who forever went on about good character and the Bible and sexual purity, the people too prudish to go dancing or wear a normal bathing suit, how did they get on board with—well, you've likely seen the lists. They were everywhere for a while. I wrote a few myself. Something like: a thrice-married, twice-divorced billionaire known for his pride, lust, anger, vanity, racism, sexism, crude language, mockery of disabled people, and rejection of God's forgiveness. How did *they* vote for *that*?

Many theories centered on an accusation of hypocrisy, which I'll consider in the next chapter. But some took a different tack. There's no contradiction here, they said: Evangelicals voted for bad things because they *like* bad things. They voted for a bad man because they already had bad ideas, bad theology, a bad way of treating people. Relatively few were willing to pull out the big guns and label evangelicalism *evil,* but that was essentially the charge.

Evangelical backing of Donald Trump "was no aberration, nor was it merely a pragmatic choice," writes Kristin Kobes Du Mez in perhaps the most-read version of this argument, *Jesus and John Wayne.* She continues in a passage worth quoting at length:

> [That support] was, rather, the culmination of evangelicals' embrace of militant masculinity, an ideology that enshrines patriarchal authority and condones the callous display of power, at home and abroad. By the time Trump arrived proclaiming himself their savior, conservative white evangelicals had already traded a faith that privileges humility and elevates "the least of these" for one that derides gentleness as the province of wusses. Rather than turning the other cheek, they'd resolved to defend their faith and their nation, secure in the knowledge that the ends justify the means. Having replaced the Jesus of the Gospels with a vengeful warrior Christ, it's no wonder many came to think of Trump in the same way. In 2016, many observers were stunned at evangelicals' apparent betrayal of their own values. In reality, evangelicals did not cast their vote despite their beliefs, but because of them.[3]

Du Mez paid attention to masculinity to a degree that others did not, and her book was a phenomenon. A *New York Times* bestseller, it became required reading in American political and evangelical circles in a way I've rarely seen.[4]

But she wasn't alone in basically applying to evangelicals Hillary Clinton's 2016 "basket of deplorables" line about "racist, sexist, homophobic, xenophobic, Islamophobic" Trump voters[5]—or Barack Obama's 2008 comment about people who "get bitter [and] cling to guns or religion or antipathy to people who aren't like them."[6] In this chapter, I'll look primarily at *Jesus and John Wayne,* but I'll also touch on Beth Allison Barr's *The Making of Biblical Womanhood* and *Becoming the Pastor's Wife.*

Because these books are closely concerned with gender roles, let me say at the outset: I'm an egalitarian. That is, I think there's strong biblical warrant for women to preach and pastor and for husbands and wives to live as peers, and I would not raise my children in a church that taught otherwise. In one important matter, then, I agree with Du Mez and Barr.

We differ in what we think it *means* that some evangelicals take the alternative stance, the complementarian or patriarchal view that only men can preach and pastor and that husbands have authority over their wives.[7]

This is a weighty debate. But any honest egalitarian must recognize that we have been in the minority—often the extreme minority—for most of church history. That doesn't prove that we're wrong, but it should be grounds for some humility, forbearance, and grace.

For the first nineteen centuries or so of Christianity, few understood men and women to be equal in the church and home. I think those generations were wrong on this point. I think they misunderstood and misapplied Scripture, sometimes catastrophically.[8] But I can hardly discard them all as evil or unfaithful. John Chrysostom, Thomas Aquinas, C. S. Lewis—surely these are not lesser Christians than me! Yet, if classed by our modern language, all these (and many, many more) were "complementarian."

It is forever tempting to make ourselves the metric of orthodoxy, benevolence, and good faith. I am staunchly egalitarian, but I know I am not that metric, and I reject the suggestion that evangelicals who disagree with me about women's roles are necessarily in thrall to a cruel, politicized chauvinism.

AFTER BEGINNING WITH Donald Trump, *Jesus and John Wayne* jumps back in time, reviewing a selection of evangelical history from the early twentieth century to the present. And, as Du Mez acknowledges, it *is* only a selection. "While dominant, the evangelical cult of masculinity does not define the whole of American evangelicalism," she writes, and "evangelical men themselves have promoted alternative models, elevating gentleness and self-control, a commitment to peace, and a divestment of power as expressions of Christian manhood."[9]

That qualification comes briefly and late, after three hundred pages on white evangelicals as a source of corruption to American democracy, an ever-lurking threat.

Du Mez's tone is consistently skeptical and deliberately adversarial.[10] She characterizes evangelicalism as a consumer culture, discounting the importance of theology and evangelicals' own accounts of our faith.[11] Here, even evangelical production and consumption of "music, news sources, books, and radio" aligning with our beliefs are suspect. Christian products are wrapped up in power.

But if we don't begin with cynicism, what exactly is wrong here? Is it bad to write books? To read them? To decorate your home with things that remind you of your faith? To listen to music with lyrics praising what you believe is true? Are we equally skeptical when progressive Christians get their news from *Sojourners* or *Slate,* or when they buy books by commentators they find worthwhile? Or is it bad only when evangelicals do it?

"Evangelical leaders bestow authority upon one another," Du Mez reveals, "blurbing each other's books, defending each other on social media, and determining which up-and-coming writers, pastors, and organizations are worthy of promotion—and which should be shunned."[12] And sure, that's all correct.

But that's not a gotcha about evangelicals. *All* authors and influencers do this. It's normal. *Du Mez* does it herself, using her successful Substack newsletter to publish excerpts from books she's endorsed, encouraging her followers to read and buy them.[13] Blurbing, recommending, and critiquing books isn't some nefarious plot by Big Evangelicalism. It's just how the book industry works in the twenty-first century. Your publisher makes you do it. In the months before this will have come out, I'll have been emailing folks asking for blurbs. That's not because I'm an evangelical. It's because the marketing team would have been unhappy with me if I didn't.

It's also worth noticing how Du Mez writes about consumption of evangelical products as a competitor to the local church. Pastors are "up against a powerful system of authority," she says, and "a few words preached on Sunday morning" just can't compete.[14]

There's a partial truth here. I wrote about it in my last book, mentioning that I'd encountered multiple pastors making an identical complaint. "The main issue I face is only having one hour a week to try to influence people," one pastor told me, "when they can get five hours a week from a TV host,

15 hours a week from a talk radio host, or many hours beyond that from a blog, YouTube channel, or online group."[15]

This is a real problem—but it's not, as Du Mez implies, that evangelicals are reading too many devotionals or listening to too much worship music. It's that, like nearly all Americans, we spend too much time on our devices, uncritically absorbing whatever social media and search engines send our way. We aren't extraordinary and militant. We're ordinary and a bit phone addled.

Moreover, Du Mez's correct recognition of the competition pastors face in discipleship undermines her broader vision of evangelicalism as a movement in misogynist lockstep. "White evangelicals are significantly more authoritarian than other religious groups," she writes early on, "and they express confidence in their religious leaders at much higher rates than do members of other faiths."[16] How authoritarian and confident are we, though, if our pastors are losing out to Instagram?

ALL THIS MAY seem like a diversion from the primary question of whether evangelicals have bad beliefs. It's not. This handling of evangelical publishing—the continued viability of which is frankly to our credit in an increasingly postliterate society—is telling. It shows the reflexive mistrust Du Mez brings to this work. That mistrust leads her to hold evangelicals to a standard she does not require of other groups and to see pervasive corruption where it doesn't exist.

In *Jesus and John Wayne,* this looks like using scare quotes to describe televangelist Jerry Falwell "getting saved" and suggesting his opposition to Soviet communism was a matter of self-dealing.[17] There are reasons to be skeptical of Falwell, sure. But can't we let him tell his testimony? And isn't it possible that he had some good, unselfish reasons to be against communist regimes that in the mid-century period were actively engaged in genocide, manufactured famine, and severe religious persecution?

This mistrust looks like repeatedly putting "family values" in scare quotes too, discounting the possibility that this idea could contain sincere concern for anything good.[18] It looks like suggesting conservative evangelicals were somehow wrong or weird for worrying over what sexual norms their children are taught in school.[19] It looks like knocking evangelicals as Islamophobic or close to it for thinking, *in the immediate post-9/11 era,* that "the threat of radical Islam loomed large"—while praising then candidate Barack Obama for "one of the most powerful speeches of his political career," in which "he denounced 'the perverse and hateful ideologies of radical Islam.' "[20]

It repeatedly looks like expecting conservative evangelicals to vote for candidates with wildly different ethical and political commitments because of a shared profession of Christianity—while making no comparable demand of progressive Christian voters. Du Mez makes this argument about both Jimmy Carter[21] and Barack Obama,[22] then triples down with Hillary Clinton:

> For white evangelicals, Clinton was on the wrong side of nearly every issue. A feminist and a career woman, she thought it took a village to raise a child. She promoted global human rights and women's rights at the expense of U.S. sovereignty, at least in the eyes of her critics. And she was pro-choice. The fact that she read the same Bible didn't register for most evangelicals, and her faith testimony came across as political pandering, or just plain lying.[23]

Can you imagine the reverse?

> *For Episcopalians, George W. Bush was on the wrong side of nearly every issue. A traditionalist whose wife's career was confined to a stereotypically feminine sphere, he emphasized the nuclear family. He promoted U.S. sovereignty even as civilian casualties mounted in Iraq and Afghanistan, at least in the eyes of his critics. And he was anti-choice. The fact that he read the same Bible didn't register for most progressive Christians, and his faith testimony came across as political pandering, or just plain lying.*

Put that way, maybe it's easier to see why voting for Clinton was always a nonstarter for many evangelicals who take life ethics seriously.

And speaking of Episcopalians and ethics, this mistrust also looks like censuring evangelicals for failing to embrace Christian pacifism and oppose the U.S. invasions of Afghanistan and Iraq[24]—while skating past the fact that mainline Protestants and Catholics also largely reject the peace tradition and gave majority support to those same invasions at their starts.[25]

I'm a Christian pacifist myself, which is a baggage-laden way of saying I can't find a way around what strikes me as straightforward biblical instruction, including directly from Jesus, for his followers to forswear violence. This is one of my most evangelical views in terms of how I got there: *The Bible says it, and I believe it, so that settles it for me.* I spent eight years in an Anabaptist church in large part because of its theology around violence, and I've written hundreds of thousands of words against U.S. military intervention in Afghanistan, Iraq, Yemen, Libya, Somalia, and beyond.

So if the argument is that all evangelicals should get on board with Christian nonviolence, great! I've been saying that forever. But going after *evangelicals alone* for rejecting pacifism, as probably 98 percent of Western Christianity has done for 1,600-odd years? Pathologizing *only evangelicals* for supporting wars that began with the endorsement of most of the American public across just about every demographic line?

No. That's not a reasonable critique.

WHEN HE SEES people leaving evangelicalism for Catholicism, Milliner told me, he wishes them well but marvels at their change of posture toward institutional failure and theological disagreement. "I am amazed," he finds himself thinking, "that all of a sudden, upon your conversion to Catholicism, you've developed this extraordinary capacity for charity to extend to your newfound home that you could not issue to your former home," to the community that birthed and nurtured your faith, the community that taught you grace and charity in the first place.[26]

Of course, the question is whether they *did* teach you grace and charity—or whether the typical evangelical experience is something more sinister, more misogynist, more like the shocking stories that pepper the pages of *Jesus and John Wayne.* This isn't a matter of *is or isn't.* I've no doubt the stories Du Mez tells are true. But the proportions are wrong, the result of a conflation of the center of evangelicalism with the fringe, the *more* with the *less.*

Here's an example. One chapter opens with an account of GodMen conferences. At these events in the early 2000s, "participants watched video clips of 'karate fights, car chases, and *Jackass*-style stunts,' offered prayers of thanks to God for their testosterone, and raised their voices in 'manly' anthems like 'Grow a Pair.' "[27]

Du Mez concedes that GodMen was one of the "more radical expressions of militant Christian masculinity," but she also describes it as "amplify[ing] trends that were becoming increasingly common in the post-9/11 era . . . making it increasingly difficult to distinguish the margins from the mainstream."[28] This all sounds weird and gross, and it comes amid a discouraging narrative on how evangelical men's culture flipped into a more aggressive, politicized mode after the 1990s.

So how big was GodMen? Was it packing out stadiums like Promise Keepers, the major evangelical men's program known for its focus on racial reconciliation?

Not quite. Contemporaneous news reports say GodMen drew a few hundred people[29] per event,[30] and the decaying remains of its website suggest the organization held fewer than ten events, all in the span of a single year, before shutting down.[31] That is, the average evangelical man in the early 2000s was *far* more likely to have mourned the evil of racism at Promise Keepers than to have sung about his testicles at GodMen.[32] Both conferences are part of evangelicalism, yes, but they're not an *equal* part. They're not comparable in influence—and it isn't hard to differentiate the two.

Du Mez makes a similar move in her handling of Doug Wilson, the Idaho pastor I mentioned in the introduction. She's not wrong that Wilson shared stages and book blurbs with more mainstream figures in the Reformed subset of evangelicalism, nor is she wrong that Wilson espouses "extreme expressions of patriarchy." But again, it's not actually "difficult to distinguish margins from mainstream."[33] Wilson is marginal. Fringe. He doesn't represent the median white evangelical (let alone evangelicals in other demographics), and he never has.

The fall of 2025 saw a whole news cycle devoted to gawking at Wilson for two reasons. One was that the secretary of defense, Pete Hegseth, attended a church in his denomination—which Wilson co-founded after not one established denomination in his Reformed tradition would tolerate him.[34]

The second reason was, well, *Wilson is fringe.* If Hegseth's denomination were the Southern Baptist Convention or the Presbyterian Church in America, both conservative and complementarian but not fringe, there'd be no story here. If Wilson were a typical evangelical, his perspective wouldn't be newsworthy. It wouldn't be the subject of a profile on CNN,[35] an interview in *The New York Times*,[36] and endless breathless tweets. Wilson shocks because he is shocking, and *that* he is shocking indicates he is far outside the evangelical norm.

IT'S WORTH NAMING that norm on the primary issue at hand. Du Mez describes a rising tide of militant evangelical masculinity in which she says the "ideological extreme [bears] a remarkable resemblance to the mainstream."[37] In *The Making of Biblical Womanhood: How the Subjugation of Women Became Gospel Truth,* Beth Allison Barr likewise presents a dire picture of evangelical gender roles, claiming that "evangelicals baptized patriarchy" and uniquely elevated it to the level of the gospel.[38]

But most American evangelicals today are egalitarians like me. They aren't on board with extreme patriarchal voices like Wilson. They aren't on board with complementarianism at all.

As the political scientist Ryan Burge has found, a strong majority of evangelicals believe women can preach—and not only to children or other women, as complementarians tend to allow. To everyone. From the pulpit. "Nearly three quarters of evangelicals agree that a properly trained and certified woman can preach on Sunday morning," Burge reported, citing national survey data.

This is a poll of self-identified evangelicals, but crucially, that pattern held across generations, church attendance rates, and views of Scripture. "Even among those who say that the Bible is literally true and attend church every week, 74 percent are in favor of women preaching," Burge wrote. "The data is basically unequivocal on this point: A majority of evangelicals favor women serving in any and all capacities in their church."[39]

There are still many evangelical complementarians, and the egalitarian majority is relatively new.[40] But perhaps it shouldn't surprise us that the movement was heading this way. After all, as historian Timothy Larsen observes, welcoming women into ministry roles including the pastorate is "a historic distinctive of evangelicalism":

> It is historic because evangelical women have been fulfilling their callings in public ministry from the founding generation of evangelicalism to the present day and in every period in between. It is a distinctive because no other large branch of the Christian family has demonstrated as long and deep a commitment to affirming the public ministries of women—not theologically liberal traditions, not Roman Catholicism or Eastern Orthodox traditions, not [Episcopalians] or other mainline Protestant traditions.

Larsen gives a litany of examples, many of them strikingly countercultural for their time. (For instance, evangelical seminaries had women on their theology faculties well before Harvard Divinity School would accept them as students.) Evangelicals have always had two ways of understanding what the Bible says about women's roles, Larsen concludes, "one that affirms and one that restricts women in public ministry."[41] Only the former is distinctly evangelical.

LARSEN'S IMPULSE TO compare is a good one because it highlights a tendency in *Jesus and John Wayne* as well as *The Making of Biblical Womanhood* to intimate that evangelicals, absent evangelicalism, would be down-the-line progressives with current-year feminist instincts. This is a mistaken notion—to put it lightly.

It's one thing to argue that evangelicalism is patriarchal, my former *Christianity Today* colleague Daniel Silliman, a historian, commented when we talked. But, he added, you should also ask: *Compared to what?* And particularly in eras past, before that egalitarian majority emerged, "most people were choosing between versions or gradations of patriarchy," Silliman said. For many, evangelicalism proved to be "actually kinder and gentler" than the way they were living before.[42]

Larsen made this point when we spoke as well. "It all depends on where you start from and how evangelicalism intersects with your life," he told me. "I'm working with somebody right now who just recently came to faith. He's incarcerated, and I can tell you his family thinks his conversion is good news."[43]

This isn't merely a matter of anecdote. *The Great Dechurching* is a 2023 book based on national, independently reviewed surveys of people who have left churches in America and those who remain in them. One set of questions asked respondents about fourteen standards and practices they "seek to follow in good faith." Some were directly religious ("pray regularly," "donate to house of worship"), but most were more generically ethical ("avoid discrimination based on race," "Providing financially and/or practically for the poor and oppressed").

You'd expect people who leave the church to stop giving it money. Of those who deconvert entirely, you'd expect lower rates of prayer or Bible reading. Sure enough, that's what the data shows. But it shows a shift on generic ethics too. On every single measure, still-churched evangelicals were markedly more likely to say they try to do the right thing: to avoid discrimination, to tangibly help immigrants and refugees, to not lie or steal or be greedy.

Granted, we don't know how well evangelicals live up to these aspirations. People lie to pollsters, often unconsciously. Nevertheless, the mere profession of commitment to these practices matters. Some 93 percent of still-churched evangelicals said they strive to avoid racist discrimination. Only 74 percent of those who've left the evangelical church said the same. The evangelicals might be misjudging themselves, but they "know the good they ought to do."[44]

In *Mere Christianity*, C. S. Lewis makes a point along these lines. You can't judge Christianity—whether as a whole or a branch of it—on the basis of Christians as you find them in a single moment in time: "Christian Miss Bates may have an unkinder tongue than unbelieving Dick Firkin. That, by itself, does not tell us whether Christianity works. The question is what Miss Bates' tongue would be like if she were not a Christian and what Dick's would be like if he became one."[45]

The question is where they started, what hands they were dealt. The question is: *Compared to what?*

Maybe evangelicals *are* more Miss Bates than Dick Firkin, though I've met too many to find that plausible. Yet even if so, we are Miss Bates *with Jesus,* and that makes a difference—a measurable difference.

Our faith has not yanked us out of our places and cultures and personalities. It hasn't made conservative white southerners cease to be conservative white southerners any more than it has sprung Larsen's friend from prison. Still, when we ask *Compared to what?* it's evident that evangelicalism makes evangelicals' ethics and behaviors better.

DU MEZ RECOGNIZES the relevance of this comparison in her book[46] and in later writing on the subject.[47] "Depending on where any given man was coming from, [complementarian] 'soft patriarchy' and 'servant leadership' might be a significant improvement over harsher authoritarian tendencies," she says in *Jesus and John Wayne.*[48] But realistic comparison tends to slip from view.

Barr's depth of knowledge on the historical subjugation of women makes her lack of illuminating comparison noteworthy too. She flattens the treatment of women across history, writing as if evangelical women in contemporary America are barely better off than our forebears in abusive, pagan societies of the ancient world. Here's one astonishing passage from *The Making of Biblical Womanhood:*

> My modern students balk at how Babylonian law allowed husbands to drown their wives for alleged adultery, but my students are also living in the state of Texas in which women make up 94 percent of the

> victims in domestic partner murder-suicides—not to mention the United States in which almost 25 percent of women have experienced severe physical violence by an intimate partner. This evidence shows not only the continuity of patriarchy from ancient Mesopotamia to modern America but also the continuity of its dark underbelly. Instead of being a point of pride for Christians, shouldn't the historical continuity of a practice that has caused women to fare much worse than men for thousands of years cause concern? Shouldn't Christians, who are called to be different from the world, treat women differently?[49]

Barr is entirely right that Christianity should make a difference in the treatment of women. In fact, *it does.* It does in the very example she gives: There's a world of difference between husbands having a legal right and social approval to drown their wives on a whim and husbands committing the universally deplored crime of murder-suicide.

Per Barr's account, if a woman ran to ye olde Babylonian police station and said, *Please help me, my husband is trying to drown me because he wrongly believes I committed adultery,* the cops would say, *Hey, she's over here, want us to give you a hand down at the lake?* If Barr's students sought law enforcement protection from a murderous husband today, whatever the defects of the Texan criminal justice system, they'd receive a completely different response.

These are not similar societies, and it is fearmongering to tell young women they are. Find me the most conservative, patriarchal, evangelical church in some remote corner of the

Texas panhandle, and I'd still bet you good money they're not down with drowning wives.

And beyond the question of whether twenty-first-century America offers a superior quality of life to ancient Babylon, this is a strange downplaying of the colossal good Christianity has done for women. As the classicist Gerald Hiestand has argued, Christianity's insistence on the equal worth of women and the equal chastity of men "has stabilized societies, granted new dignity and opportunities to women, and has penalized (and continues to penalize) powerful men for tyrannical sexual behavior."[50]

To give just one illustrative detail: In pre-Christian Rome, women were not granted individual names. Fathers—patriarchs—just slapped a feminine suffix on the family name and called it a day. In a house with multiple daughters, then, they might all be named the same thing, distinguished only by birth order ("the elder," "the second," and so on), as if it would be simply too much trouble to take thirty seconds to notice each infant girl as her own human being.[51]

We do not act this way today. We do not think this way today. So comprehensive has been Christianity's transformation of Western women's lives, even where a degree of patriarchy persists, that "any condemnation of Christianity as patriarchal and repressive [is now] derived from a framework of values that [is] itself utterly Christian," historian Tom Holland observes in *Dominion: How the Christian Revolution Remade the World.* "That every human being possessed an equal dignity was not remotely a self-evident truth [before Christ]. A Roman would have laughed at it," and it is because of Christianity that we no longer laugh.[52]

I share Barr's theology of women's roles, down to the

specific interpretations she gives on some key passages of Scripture.[53] I appreciate her desire to reform evangelicalism rather than discard it. She writes in a mood of hope that some comparable authors lack.[54] Yet her assertion that, in how they treat women, present-day complementarian evangelicals look "just like everyone else" in the "continuous story of patriarchy—of women suppressed, oppressed, devalued, and silenced" *since the ancient world* is nonsensical and ahistorical.[55] Even Doug Wilson's daughters have a podcast.

THE MAKING OF *Biblical Womanhood* is rife with material that undercuts its sweeping declarations about evangelical oppression of women and distortion of the gospel. As Barr's own review shows, Christianity affirmed and enforced the value of women in a world that despised us, and evangelicalism is the major branch of the church most distinguished by its welcome of women to the pastorate and other positions of authority.

Still, large swathes of evangelicalism are complementarian, and many critics want to tie their beliefs to abuse. Du Mez gestures to a series of evangelical sex scandals in the first quarter of this century, then says:

> Many of the men implicated in the abuse, or in covering up cases of abuse, were the same men who had been preaching militant masculinity, patriarchal authority, and female purity and submission. The frequency of these instances, and the tendency of evangelicals to diminish or dismiss cases of abuse in their own communities, suggests that evangelicals' response to allegations of abuse in the era of Trump cannot be explained by political expediency alone.

> Rather, these tendencies appear to be endemic to the movement itself.[56]

This is a big claim, and in this paragraph, it's supported by a single cited source. That source is a blog post by a writer named Kathryn Joyce pointing to an essay she published at *The American Prospect,* a progressive magazine. Unfortunately, the essay cannot bear the weight of Du Mez's claim.

Joyce does criticize the handling of abuse reports by the administration of the historically fundamentalist Bob Jones University. But she also reports that the wider Bob Jones community was agitating for transparency and accountability, and the administration complied. The school brought in a respected abuse investigation firm, "an independent group of evangelical lawyers, pastors, and psychologists" run by Billy Graham's grandson, Boz Tchividjian, who at that point taught law at the conservative evangelical Liberty University.

Broadening her scope to the rest of evangelicalism, Joyce's findings are similarly mixed. She describes other "allegations of sex abuse, rape, and harassment—and a culture that has badly mishandled them," in some cases attributing these ills to a "victim-blaming emphasis on women's purity."

But she also finds many evangelicals trying to do right, including major organizations like the relief ministry Samaritan's Purse and the Southern Baptist Convention. And then there's Tchividjian himself, who doesn't blame the abuse he's spent years investigating on evangelical theology. The dynamic he sees in the field is evangelicals being too trusting and gracious as well as inexperienced in these matters and inclined to save face for the sake of the gospel.[57] That last bit doesn't reflect well on us, but the problem it identifies is not beliefs about sex.

BARR MATCHES DU Mez's enthusiasm for linking evangelical beliefs to abuse. In her second book, *Becoming the Pastor's Wife: How Marriage Replaced Ordination as a Woman's Path to Ministry,* she sees herself telling a "story connecting the dots between a gender theology that rejects women's independent pastoral authority and a culture that privileges male clergy over clergy abuse victims."[58] Sex abuse scandals in complementarian institutions, she says, "are the product of a systemic culture teaching that women are worth less than men."[59]

There are cases, undoubtedly, where this connection may be fairly made, and each one is a horror. Still, the question of proportions—of what's typical in evangelicalism and how that compares to the general population—remains.

Most evangelicals, remember, are no longer complementarian, and Barr herself raises doubts about how many of the remaining complementarians have real hierarchy in their marriages. She cites complementarian insiders[60] and sociological sources alike to suggest that modern evangelical patriarchy is softening and declining.[61]

Moreover, by any measure, American evangelicalism is a movement of tens of millions, and abuse cases in our churches can be *too common* without actually being *common.* They are *too common* if they happen at all, and they do. But *common*?

We've all seen the headlines, and many of us know a real-life story or two, with varying degrees of severity and personal proximity. Yet some rough calculations from demographer Lyman Stone, who does quantitative research on human population and behavior patterns, suggest evangelical abuse scandals are, thank God, pretty thin on the ground. They are not the majority report.

Stone looked at a major abuse investigation report released in 2022 by the Southern Baptist Convention (SBC), the largest evangelical denomination in America. It was an "awful damning report," he said, and it identified 409 SBC-affiliated people accused of abuse.[62] That's a lot. But once Stone put that figure in the context of how many men would've worked at about forty-five thousand SBC churches in America[63]—plus the overall rate at which American men commit sexual abuse—his napkin math indicted that the abuse rate for men in SBC ministry was actually quite *low,* perhaps a tenth of the American male average.[64]

Stone was careful to flag the limits of his calculations. These are estimates. Yet, he added, it's "difficult to imagine a way to get the SBC stats above the general-male-population stats."[65]

Then came the big reveal: Per the SBC report, that 409 number was accused abusers "believed to be SBC-affiliated *at some point in time*" (emphasis mine). When the investigators went over that list, however, and "conducted significant research to assess whether any of the alleged abusers were still associated with an SBC church," they found just nine were in any kind of active ministry, and only *two* of those were active in the SBC.[66]

Even two verified abusers in active ministry would be too many, and that small number doesn't negate the grave scandals in the report. It does suggest, however, that abuse in this sprawling, complementarian denomination, though *too common,* is also *uncommon.*

ONE FINAL NOTE on this matter, beginning with a point made to me by Molly Worthen. She's a University of North Carolina historian whose work on American evangelicalism is fascinating both in its own right and because Worthen converted into evangelical Christianity as an adult and an accomplished academic.

Something "I've been pondering for a while," Worthen said in our interview, "is that in the context of secularization, fewer and fewer Americans are really plugged into—and feel connected to and implicated in—the sins and the achievements of institutions and big communities." Institutions magnify human power. We can do more in groups with rules and resources than we can do individually: more good, and also more evil.

As America has become less religious, Worthen observed, we've lost our links to institutions, but we've lost them asymmetrically. Now, "conservative religious people, whether Catholic or Protestant, are more connected to institutions that are able—simply by their size and by the reality of institutions—to do bad things on a bigger scale," including sexual abuse and cover-ups. These institutional sins deserve condemnation and require reform, but a correct response also means understanding that "this kind of bad behavior is what comes with institutions."[67]

Or, as a Vancouver youth pastor named Lexi put it to me, "People say absence makes the heart grow fonder, but it's actually kind of the opposite: If you distance yourself from church community, church community is going to look uglier and uglier the further away you get. But the second you step into a healthy church community—I mean, it's not perfect, but a good church community, you see, *Oh yeah, these people are broken, but it's not bad like I thought.*"[68]

In this sense, the evangelical church is a lot like the family. Abuse happens in this context, absolutely. It's painful and destructive for victims and entire communities. Read enough true stories of familial abuse and you may begin to think these tendencies are endemic to the institution.[69] Likewise, Larsen said to me, "I check three or four religion news sites almost every day, and what I get every day are stories exposing anyone who's been in ministry and has sexually violated anybody. Reading these stories over and over, it changes your perception."

"But then," he continued, "I remind myself: This is not my experience of church. And I talk to people in more conservative parts of the country, and I say, 'Tell me what's going on in your church.' And they say, 'We just try to love each other. It's just normal.' "[70]

ARE EVANGELICAL BELIEFS bad? No, they're not.

Of course, I have my differences with many evangelicals, just as I do with Catholic and Orthodox Christians, none of whom allow women in the priesthood. But even where I think other evangelicals are getting it wrong, my answer is the same: Evangelicalism is well within the bounds of historic-orthodox Christianity. Roles of women have been a subject of earnest internal conversation for decades, and our sexual ethics (which I'll address more directly in chapter 4) are not outlandish by any standard except that of left-of-center Westerners in the last fifteen years. Evangelical faith is just normal. Evangelical people are just folks.

A movement this size inevitably contains evil and excess. There are some disgusting evangelical misogynists out there, people who almost make Doug Wilson look like a cuddly moderate. You can find many stories of abuse, and I have no interest in downplaying that reality. That scandal coming to mind right now? I also think it's bad. Every one of those cases is an injustice for the victims and an affront to Christ.

But authoritarianism and abuse are not the sum of the movement—far from it. They are not its essence. And funnily enough, an important piece of evidence on this comes from Du Mez herself.

Evangelicals—"including white, evangelical, complementarian men"—read *Jesus and John Wayne* vociferously, she said on the five-year anniversary of its release. They read it "in good faith," and they recommended it to their friends. Then they invited Du Mez on their podcasts. "I like to joke that if there is a white evangelical man who doesn't have a podcast, I haven't met him." She continued:

> I did so many podcasts that first year, I lost track. At first, I braced myself each time for harsh critique, but one after another hosted me with curiosity and grace. They were ready to rethink things. They were opening the door to me into their communities. They were sharing their platforms, and, as trusted authority figures, they were telling people to read the book despite what they may have heard. They did not do this without risk. I have heard of at least two who lost their jobs in part for taking this risk. To all of these men—dozens of them—I owe a debt of gratitude for the book's success.[71]

This isn't a one-off comment. Du Mez has repeatedly expressed her gratitude to these readers. Reflecting to her college's student paper, she described being "struck by how many evangelical leaders are reaching out to me and thanking me" and expressed amazement at "the humility with which the book is being received in these circles."[72]

In fact, the "book's biggest fans are evangelicals themselves, and many conservative white evangelicals who are able to receive this book with incredible humility and introspection," Du Mez said on a podcast. "It really has been those conservative evangelicals, including a ton of conservative white evangelical men, who have promoted this book in their own spaces, through their little podcasts, through church Bible studies, through pastors' groups, just bringing it to others and saying, 'Hey guys, we have to read this.' "[73]

This reception undercuts the thesis of *Jesus and John Wayne.* It may not be too much to say this reception *disproves* the thesis, because it sounds a lot like Jesus—and not much like John Wayne. It sounds like an eagerness for self-examination, for accountability, for repentance where needed, and not at all like the "militant masculinity" that "condones the callous display of power," that Du Mez describes in that long quote I shared at the start of this chapter.[74]

"By the time Trump arrived proclaiming himself their savior, conservative white evangelicals had already traded a faith that privileges humility and elevates 'the least of these' for one that derides gentleness as the province of wusses," Du Mez charges in that passage. But conservative white evangelicals, in her own phrase, received her book with "incredible humility," even at serious cost to themselves.

"Rather than turning the other cheek," she alleges in that same part, "they'd resolved to defend their faith and their nation, secure in the knowledge that the ends justify the means." But when *Jesus and John Wayne* critiqued their faith and their nation in unsparing terms, their reaction was to promote it in their churches and share it with their friends. They greeted her accusations with, again in her phrase, "curiosity and grace."

Du Mez would likely note that not all evangelicals met her book this way. True enough. I've seen uncharitable responses online. Not all evangelicals are humble. Some are proud, angry, chauvinist. There are a lot of evangelicals out there. And a remarkable number of them—conservative, complementarian, white evangelical men, many of them likely Trump voters—took Du Mez's slap on the right cheek and turned to her the other cheek also.

CHAPTER THREE

HYPOCRISY

Fine, maybe the beliefs are good, but evangelicals betray them all the time.

"IT'S NOT LIKE I'm not in love with Trump," Jane explained, leaning forward for emphasis. "There were some choices to be made. There were some trajectories that I was like, *This is scary to me for the future. And that seems like, in the grand scheme of things, a better option.*"

We were sitting in her husband's office at their Dallas-area church. It's an evangelical, Spanish-language congregation composed almost entirely of first- and second-generation immigrants. Most of those who aren't U.S. citizens are in the country illegally, and most of those who are citizens voted for Donald Trump. By the time we sat down for an interview after the service, the building was emptying out following a lunch of chicken tortas.

"I don't know. It's become such a thing, about how you voted," Jane continued. "But maybe most people are just kind of silently thinking, *Hey, I don't really want to go this way, and that's the other option, and let's see what God does.* Because, honestly, I just go, *God, I don't even know what's going on*—but I do feel more comfortable for my children right now, with Trump, because I'm not having the same bombardment of sexualized content that I was. Even if it's just that for right now, I'm thankful."

Thinking back to 2016, Jane described her initial decision to support Trump as a pragmatic settling, but a settling she doesn't regret given the policies at stake. "I think because of who he was up against, it was mostly voting *against* Hillary Clinton," she told me. "Because there were two options there—or not voting, or voting independent—but two real options. And imagining a future with Hillary as president was just too unbearable."

All three times Trump ran, Jane said, her calculation was pretty much the same. She didn't trust that Hillary Clinton, Joe Biden, or Kamala Harris would "honor the family unit. I would say, as a mom, that's probably my biggest thing in voting," particularly since the introduction of trans bathroom bills and policies (saying transgender people could use facilities matching their felt identity rather than their biological sex) beginning around 2016. "It has felt like: *Here, you have to accept this.* I'm like, *No, I don't want to accept that. Can you just let me be?*"

"For me," Jane reiterated, the biggest question in voting is: "What environment is going to protect the innocence of my children?" And in that regard, she said, the current Democratic Party's policies are intolerable, even if the very imperfect alternative is Trump.[1]

JANE'S CHURCH IS almost entirely Hispanic, and her husband is an immigrant from Mexico. But Jane herself is white, one of the 81 percent of white evangelical voters who went for Trump in 2016, and one of an increasingly racially diverse group of evangelicals who backed him at a similar rate in 2020 and

2024. That is, she's the kind of evangelical who comes under the allegation I'll consider in this chapter: hypocrisy.

The idea here is not that evangelicalism isn't really about beliefs, nor is it that our beliefs are bad. It's that the beliefs are good, but we betray them all the time.

All that stuff about character, virtue, and ultimate answerability to God—right out the window when Trump showed up. There was evidence of this in the past, in evangelical behavior with other favored politicians and in our record on race. But, this charge says, Trump has made it unmistakable: Evangelicals claim to follow a God who tells us to love our neighbor, but when the chance came to have a political champion, we dropped all that to embrace a cruel and racist bully.

I've made a version of this allegation myself,[2] and many others have too.[3] In *Jesus and John Wayne,* Kristin Kobes Du Mez notes that in 2011, pollsters found "only 30 percent of white evangelicals believed that 'a person who commits an "immoral" act could behave ethically in a public role.' The month before the [2016] election, 72 percent believed this was possible"—convenient, to say the least.[4]

"Why is it that Christianity seems impotent to deal radically, and therefore effectively, with the issues of discrimination and injustice on the basis of race?" asked Cheryl J. Sanders, a pastor and professor of Christian ethics at Howard University, in a 2020 essay for *Christianity Today.* It's not "due to a basic weakness" in Christianity, she answered, but because "we have betrayed the genius of our religion."[5]

"Because evangelicals in the case of Bill Clinton so heavily stressed the importance of upright character as a qualification for holding the office of president, there's no defense for evangelicals who fall back to making what they believe is the best choice between two bad options—supporting a candidate like

Donald Trump," wrote Aaron Renn in *Life in the Negative World,* which I'll engage further in chapter 4. "Any support looks like hypocrisy."[6]

But perhaps the single most prominent hypocrisy accusation comes from a journalist named Tim Alberta. His 2023 book, *The Kingdom, the Power, and the Glory: American Evangelicals in an Age of Extremism,* was a runaway success, and it stood apart from other Trump-era volumes on evangelical politics for two reasons.

One is that Alberta is the real deal as a shoe-leather reporter: He travels and interviews, observes and cross-examines. The other is that he's the son of an evangelical pastor who remains a practicing Christian. He doesn't write about evangelicals like a zoologist encountering a strange new species in the forest. He's critical but never contemptuous.

Alberta describes Trump as a "lecherous, impenitent scoundrel" who's "transformed *evangelical* from spiritual signifier into political punch line, exposing the selective morality and ethical inconsistency and rank hypocrisy" of the movement.[7] And it's not hard to find prominent evangelicals who reversed themselves on the importance of personal character and faith in 2016.

Take the late James Dobson, evangelical parenting guru and pundit. In 1998, after then President Bill Clinton was exposed in adultery, he wrote that "character DOES matter. You can't run a family, let alone a country, without it."[8] In 2016—as Trump insulted his way to the GOP nomination, building on a foundation of fame acquired posing for *Playboy* and cheating on his wives—Dobson was all out of fire and brimstone. He implausibly described Trump as "a baby Christian"[9] and "tender to things of the Spirit."[10]

Or there's Dallas megachurch pastor Robert Jeffress. In

2012, he tried to rally evangelicals against Republican candidate Mitt Romney because of his Mormonism, slamming leaders who "for the last eight years of the Bush administration have been telling us how important it is to have an evangelical Christian in office who reads his Bible every day, and now suddenly these same leaders are telling us that a candidate's faith really isn't that important."[11] A mere four years later, Jeffress was saying that a candidate's faith sometimes is "not the most important consideration," especially when you need to elect "the meanest, toughest, son-of-a-you-know-what."[12]

As I said, I've made this charge myself, and out of all the critiques of evangelicalism I'm interrogating, hypocrisy is the one to which I'm most sympathetic. There's something here, and it hits hardest on race and on Trump, particularly regarding his personal character.

I'VE NOT CHANGED my mind about Trump, but I've come to see the story is more complicated than I once thought. One complication is the not-quite-reality of that 81 percent figure, which I could challenge on several grounds. I could mention that about 40 percent of evangelicals don't vote in any given presidential race, and that when you factor that in, backing Trump is a minority choice even among white evangelicals.[13]

Or I could mention that the 81 percent is statistically identical to white evangelical votes for the GOP nominee in every election this century.[14] "The problem with voting is it's a binary choice," political scientist Ryan Burge told me. "And a lot of evangelicals vote for Trump. But they would vote for McCain, they would vote for Romney, they would vote for—put a Republican in the Republican spot and they would vote for them."[15]

Or that a vote may be conflicted, but you can't see that anguish in the exit polls. Taylor, the indecisive Pennsylvania voter I introduced in chapter 1, said the 2024 race was "two bad options. It's like, *Do you want your right leg chopped off or your left leg chopped off?* I want to not chop off either."[16]

Or that white evangelicals didn't easily warm up to Trump in 2016, initially preferring rivals like Ted Cruz.[17] When Trump became the presumptive nominee, the only viable alternative to Clinton, it's true that evangelical Republicans fell in line. Yet they were slow on the uptake, "skeptical of Trump even as late as April 2016, well into primary season," as Pew Research Center reported at the time.[18]

Or I could mention that a mere 2 percent of white evangelicals told Pew that they'd heard a pro-Trump message from their clergy in 2016.[19] Or that a 2020 Pew analysis of hundreds of sermons found pulpit endorsements were exceedingly rare in white evangelicalism.[20] Or that a 2022 Pew survey further found that most white evangelicals and black Protestants alike oppose pulpit endorsements.[21]

And, okay, now I *have* mentioned all that, because I think it's worth mentioning and not dismissing as "evangelical gerrymandering," as per Du Mez.[22] But I'm not going to spend further time on this, because it's undeniable that a huge part of American evangelicalism *does* back Trump. That's the part at issue here.

BEYOND HYPOCRISY, ALBERTA'S basic charges in *The Kingdom, the Power, and the Glory* are political idolatry and expediency. He favorably quotes a pastor saying that what's wrong with American evangelicals is "America. Too many of them worship America."[23]

And in that worship, Alberta writes, they've become "menacing and extreme." They've moved beyond "winning elections and preserving the culture" to "destroying enemies and dominating the country by any means necessary. There was no rhetoric too appalling, no alliance too shady, no biblical application too sacrilegious."[24] They've gone spiritually bankrupt, he alleges, willing to defend the indefensible in politics even as they'd condemn it in every other part of life.[25]

Most of Alberta's book isn't argument but narrative. He travels the country, meeting evangelicals who love Trump and evangelicals who vehemently oppose him. He profiles pastors who begin each sermon with furious political commentary and pastors who disciple their flocks in Christian nonviolence and eschewal of political might. He lifts many rocks and finds many creepy-crawlies, Christians willing to say all kinds of wild things on record.

Much as in the last chapter, however, we must ask about proportions. For example, Alberta profiles an inflammatory Tennessee pastor named Greg Locke, a mainstay of media attention to Trumpist evangelicals. Locke has been covered by *The New York Times, The Atlantic,* CNN, PBS, MSNBC, the BBC, Reuters, *The Guardian,* Yahoo, *The Washington Post, Newsweek,* NOTUS, *Daily Mail,* Vice, *The Daily Beast, MinistryWatch, The Tennessean,* Baptist News Global, Media Matters for America, *The Independent, Politico, The Christian Post, The Daily Dot, ChurchLeaders,* and more.

But is Locke the *norm*? Is his church what *most* evangelical churches—or even most predominantly white and politically right-wing evangelical churches—are like?

No. Not even close.

In angrier passages, Alberta argues that Locke and others of his ilk are increasingly typical. Locke's antics "would come as a shock to many self-respecting Christians who still want to believe that their pastors are nothing like Locke; that their churches are nothing like [his] Global Vision; that they themselves are nothing like the people in that tent." He writes:

> These self-respecting Christians are in denial. It's easy for evangelicals to dismiss Global Vision as an outlier, the same way they did Westboro Baptist. It's much harder to scrutinize the extremism that has infiltrated their own churches. . . . Just as with our politics, there is no longer a clear line of demarcation between the fringe and the mainstream. Ten years ago, Global Vision would have been considered a cult. Today, Locke preaches to 2.2 million Facebook followers and poses alongside Franklin Graham at the White House.[26]

Alarm at the prospect of one's own church becoming like Locke's is justifiable—but the justification here is pretty thin.

By Alberta's own account, Locke is a knowledgeable and persuasive preacher of Scripture when he stays off politics.[27] His politicking is incendiary, demagogic, and grossly inappropriate in church, yet Alberta shares no evidence of the characteristic control and exploitation of a cult. Locke comes off as undisciplined and opportunistic, but more cowardly than coercive. He seems to be a man—in Alberta's view, and mine too—making grave mistakes, but also a man for whom the gospel has been legitimately transformative after a youth of violence and crime.[28] (Again: *Compared to what?*)

And most of all, Locke comes off as fringe. White House photo ops or not, there's a reason he shows up again and again (and again) in reports on evangelical extremism. There's a reason Alberta traveled to Tennessee to meet him instead of popping into any random evangelical church: The overwhelming odds are that the random church would be normal. Which is to say, nothing like Locke.

AT MANY POINTS throughout *The Kingdom, the Power, and the Glory,* Alberta seems to recognize this truth. He positively quotes Southern Baptist author Dan Darling—who lived in Locke's town for years—expressing frustration that "crazy stuff" distracts from ordinary church life and extraordinary charity work.

"We have people on the ground everywhere. I mean, literally anywhere you see human suffering, you see Southern Baptists, you see evangelicals," Darling tells Alberta. In that Tennessee town, evangelicals "had done heroic work in the community, including starting a public-private cooperative to help feed, clothe, and educate underserved youth. They got no coverage from the Nashville press—and they didn't want any. 'But when Greg Locke starts spouting all this crazy nonsense,'" Darling said, "'guess who makes the cover of *The Tennessean*?'"[29]

Occasionally, Alberta explicitly rejects the idea that "most evangelicals are craven hypocrites" who "only pretend to care about righteousness when it suits their political interests."[30] There are "thousands of healthy, vibrant churches across this country," he says,[31] and "millions of Christians in America . . . follow [Christ's commands of love] with rigor," though the "public doesn't see their support of single moms or their donations to African clean-water initiatives."[32]

Moreover, political crazy doesn't always preclude serious, tangible faithfulness. "I talk with church leaders regularly," an evangelical seminary professor tells Alberta early in the book, "and what they've said to me is, 'Some of the people in our churches who have lost the [political] plot—or, in some cases, downright lost their minds—they're the ones giving the most time to the homeless shelter down the street. They're the ones coming here on the weekends to cook meals for hungry people.' "

A pastor who had right-wing congregants accost and harass him over politics agrees. "Here's the thing. I always figured it was five percent that was crazy—no more than that," he said to Alberta. "We have a lot of strong Christians here. Some of them like Trump; some of them might be worked up about [critical race theory] or whatever else. But they would never do that crazy stuff."[33]

"These are good people," the professor added. "They have the Father's heart. They want to be like Jesus. But they've lost their way a little bit. We need to bring them back."[34]

FOR ALL THAT, Alberta reports some truly appalling stories and finishes his research clearly discouraged, convinced that "most Christians in America" are "captive to a cultural religion" decidedly unlike Christ. Locke's style, he says, is evangelicalism's "new normal."[35]

I understand why Alberta comes to that conclusion. At times, I've come close to it in my writing, and many of the heroes of Alberta's tale—evangelical pastors and writers like Brian Zahnd, Russell Moore, David French, and Dan Darling—are people I've met, worked with, or read appreciatively. They're people whose rejection of Trump I share and whose skepticism of Christian pursuit of power I usually exceed.

And yet—and yet—the people in the pews. They have their foibles and sins, of course—as do we all—and some aren't politically sophisticated. But neither are they the hypocrites they've been made out to be. They aren't cunning and Machiavellian. More often they're bewildered by rapid changes in American society and trying to do the right thing with the tiny amount of political responsibility and energy they have.[36] They're less like Locke than Jane.

BEFORE I MOVE on from hypocrisy about Trump to hypocrisy about race, two quick points. First, I want to distinguish between evangelical elites—famous pastors, activists, and influencers—and ordinary evangelicals. With Alberta, I want to say there's a difference between "people who knew better" and "those who did not."[37]

The raging politico who can't seem to log off and love his neighbor has become a stock character of American politics. But there's another character far better represented in our democracy: the party-line voter (and sometimes nonvoter) who really does intend to do her civic duty but just has so much else to do first. There's dinner to cook, laundry to sort, email to answer, a dog to wash. This is many evangelicals in the 81 percent.[38]

In that sense, evangelical support for Trump was at once a very big deal and a comparatively small one. It was big when done by evangelical elites, the kind of people (and in some cases, like Dobson, the *exact* people) who spent the 1990s putting out statements about character, then shut up for Trump. The book of James warns that those "who teach will be judged more strictly," and I think high-profile evangelical Trump supporters taught badly and knew better.[39]

Yet many ordinary voters knew rather less. I'll never forget mentioning Trump's *Access Hollywood* tape to an older evangelical relative in 2016. This was the recording in which he boasted about grabbing women's genitalia, and I said I couldn't believe people still supported him after hearing what he'd said. She said she hadn't heard of it at all. That was the first time I'd have an exchange about Trump along those lines. It wasn't the last.

I still think voting for Trump was a mistake, but I know many evangelicals who think otherwise, and they're not unprincipled hacks. They're also not James Dobson. They're not Robert Jeffress. The grand total of three minutes they spent voting for Trump in 2016, 2020, and 2024 is not even close to the sum of their lives, faith, and character.

SECOND, RECALL HOW Jane described herself as intensely worried about trans issues. She also cited abortion as a longstanding and unique concern. This is how many evangelical voters think, and it's a major factor in a coherent formula that ends with a Trump vote. I'm not positing a *reluctant voter* thesis (which may have been common in the spring of 2016 but has since faded) so much as a *moral obligation voter* thesis.

It works like this: Start with a strong theological, ethical, and therefore political stance on trans issues and abortion.[40] (As far back as 1976, *Christianity Today* was affirming that the "Bible stands absolutely against the killing of fetal life," and that among "Bible-believing theologians" this "issue is no longer in dispute.")[41] Add the common notion that voting is an American duty and abstention amounts to irresponsible apathy. Then layer on top the reality that a third-party candidate can't win. Put all that together and what you get is a Trump vote.

This isn't my personal voting math. But it is the math for

a lot of people, and it's an understandable, reasonable, and morally defensible decision.

Du Mez and others have argued that it's a "myth" that "opposition to abortion drives evangelical politics."[42] If so, somebody should tell evangelicals, because they seem pretty sure that abortion matters deeply.[43] It may not always be the top-of-mind priority—right now, trans issues seem more urgent, and jobs and tax rates are often pressing—but it's a constant. It's a screener for every candidate, much as belief in the threat of climate change is for many progressives.[44]

Between 2016 and 2026, many prominent Democratic politicians moved well to the left on abortion and trans issues. Hillary Clinton in 2016 tossed out "safe, legal, and rare" as an abortion slogan to take a hardline pro-choice position, even approving abortions of babies developed enough to survive outside the womb without medical aid.[45] Her party has turned off many people, not only evangelicals, with its ambient hostility toward religion and its alignment with LGBTQ activists at the expense of religious liberty.[46]

"I voted in a different way from most evangelicals," Michael Wear, who did faith outreach for Obama's 2008 campaign, said to me in an interview. "But you have to acknowledge that the Democratic candidates after 2016 didn't even *ask* for their vote. In fact," he went on:

> Democrats were openly saying that if they won, it would be a victory over white evangelicals. That was the explicit narrative. We saw books with titles like *White Too Long.* Can you name *any* community that would not react? That would vote for someone who is not just indifferent towards them, but is trying to

> gain credibility with other constituencies by opposing them?[47]

What I've described here is the kind of thinking I heard from evangelicals across my interviews and research.

Rogerio, who works at the immigration advocacy center, "cannot vote the other way," he said when we talked. "I cannot vote for a party who openly goes for abortion. I cannot vote for a lot of the things that they value. I cannot. Biblically, it is not possible." Rogerio doesn't like everything about Trump and the GOP, he said, and he understands that other faithful Christians vote differently. He's not sure he's in the right. But for now, on "abortion and also same-sex marriage and trans" issues, the Democratic Party is impossible to support.[48]

Megan Basham, a right-wing evangelical journalist, takes this same position in her book. "Clinton and Biden promised voters that electing them would allow the butchery [of abortion] to continue," she writes, and evangelicals simply believed them. "Thanks to the single-issue voters who cast ballots for Donald Trump, tens of thousands of babies are alive today who otherwise would have been fed to the abortion machine."[49]

"If I have any issue that determines my vote," Reformed theologian R. C. Sproul said in 2020, "it's abortion. Because any candidate who supports abortion by law has completely abrogated his responsibility . . . to protect and maintain the sanctity of human life. So I will not *ever* vote for any candidate in any office—including dogcatcher—who is pro-abortion."[50]

Or there's Glenn, a retired pastor and businessman in the Pittsburgh area. He described life issues as "very important" to him: abortion and euthanasia. "If there was somebody that was going to push something like that that was so counter to my core beliefs, I could not vote for that person," he told me. "I think that if I read the Scriptures correctly, these are the things that God judges the country on. So for me, they matter greatly."

Glenn believes voting is a duty and that third-party votes are unwise given how our elections are structured. Trump for him was "the lesser of two evils" in a system that "does not regurgitate up the best of us to leadership positions."

"And by the way," he made sure to say as our interview wound down, "I think Donald Trump's a cad."[51]

BUT ENOUGH ABOUT Trump. Evangelicals in America, as *Christianity Today* said in 1968, have a "racial paralysis."

That declaration came in the review of a slim book by a black evangelical named William E. Pannell. "A stinging and slashing attack on white complacency, hypocrisy, paternalism, and smugness," the unsigned *Christianity Today* article said, "the book sharply attacks white evangelicals in particular for failing to practice what Jesus taught. How can men who claim to follow Christ so blatantly deny the clear teachings of the Gospel?"[52]

Pannell's book, *My Friend, the Enemy,* is indeed strongly worded. It's also beautiful, a master class in spare and stunning rhetoric, at once gutting and funny, desperate and sad. And unfortunately, nearly six decades post-release, much of it feels current.

Black and white evangelicals' "devotion to each other" today is "tentative and halting," just as Pannell said then.[53] We believe the same things and worship the same God, but so often we do so separately, and too often we—those of us who are white, that is—aren't sure what to think or do about that.

(The same can sometimes be said about white evangelicals and other groups, but black-white relations are more prominent in American history and evangelical thought, so it's where I'll focus here.)

"Though we are displaying some indications of guilt over the sins of our fathers," Pannell acknowledged, race remains "the historic blind spot in our vision." We can "get men to God, but not to each other."[54]

I DON'T MEAN to suggest there's no difference between the 1960s and the 2020s. On the contrary, reading *My Friend, the Enemy* and other works sketching American racial history—like Anthea Butler's *White Evangelical Racism* and Jemar Tisby's *The Color of Compromise,* to which I'll turn soon—I'm struck by the change at least as much as the continuity.

Work remains to be done on race in the U.S. church. But a century ago, the American South was run by white terrorists.[55] The murder of Emmett Till and the Birmingham church bombing happened in my parents' lifetimes. Whatever our failings and sins on race, even in the South, the average white evangelical is not like *that* anymore, thank God.

Likewise, Pannell writes of evangelical moderates who thought it "best that I not live within the limits" of their towns.[56] They might have affirmed that black Americans should have equal rights before the law (eventually), but they didn't want black neighbors on their block or black friends in their living rooms, and they certainly didn't want black sons-in-law married to their white daughters.[57]

This too is mercifully unfamiliar among white evangelicals now. I've seen the shift on interracial marriage myself: I know white evangelicals who were uncomfortable with it in the

1990s but would meet an interracial couple with unqualified enthusiasm today.

And granted, the change here is not always a matter of virtue. Too many white evangelicals came to recognize the right thing only *after* the law required it. Even so, the change is real, and in younger generations, many of us never knew anything else.

This pairing of change and continuity is what I want to address here. Evangelical hypocrisy on race is, to my mind, the most compelling of the charges on our docket, exceeding even the charge of hypocrisy about Trump. Yet even a strong case may be pressed too far. A prosecutor who goes for murder when he should have sought a conviction for manslaughter may end up with no conviction at all. I believe we *do* need fresh conviction on interracial unity in the church, so I want to get the charges right.

BUTLER'S APPROACH IS prosecutorial maximalism. "Racism is a feature, not a bug, of American evangelicalism," she declares in *White Evangelical Racism: The Politics of Morality in America.*[58] Indeed, she argues, evangelicalism *is* white racism. It's "a nationalistic political movement whose purpose is to support the hegemony of white Christian men over and against the flourishing of others."[59] Even now, "slavery and racism permeate evangelicalism," Butler contends, and for evangelicals, "Christianity is whiteness as well as belief."[60]

We might say our faith is about Jesus, the Bible, service, and so on, but Butler rejects all that. Evangelicalism is about Republican politics and race, she announces—because media says so: "This is the working definition of American evangelicalism. American print and television media have embraced and promoted this definition, and the American public has accepted it."[61] (Print *and* television, you say? Oh, well, in that case . . .)

In her introduction, Butler strikes an almost mournful tone when she asks, "Does being evangelical really mean being white?" Her answer is yes—"Evangelicalism is synonymous with whiteness"—but then, of course it is: She'd already said evangelical means white seven pages prior. And remember, this is true on the word of "the media, the general public, and politicians," noted religious authorities all.[62]

Not only is racism foundational and integral to evangelicalism, Butler says, it's somehow getting *worse.* She writes that, since 1968, "evangelical ideas and beliefs about race [began] to harden."[63] Since 2000, it's become impossible to "wav[e] away through belief, theology, and denial" the "racism that underlay [evangelicals'] religious movement."[64] And since 2008 and the election of Barack Obama, evangelicals have indulged in "much more virulent, in-your-face racism."[65]

This would be horrifying were it true. But the thrust of history pushes against Butler's wholesale pessimism. Take 2008, for instance. It's a minor detail, but Obama "succeeded in chiseling off small but significant chunks of white evangelical voters" from the GOP, *The New York Times* reported soon after his victory. In fact, "Obama doubled his support among young white evangelicals (those ages 18 to 29) compared with [the white candidate John Kerry in 2004]. The increase was almost the same for white evangelicals ages 30 to 44."[66] Is that evidence of racism getting worse?

Or look at the years between 1968 and the present. The white evangelical record here is far from pristine—but it's also far from regressive.[67] This is a span in which white evangelicals gradually embraced desegregation, belatedly approved of the civil rights movement, issued a number of institutional and individual apologies for past racism, and launched large-scale efforts to promote racial reconciliation.[68] We've made real progress in this time.

I don't say pure progress or smooth progress or consistent progress. We're often two steps forward, one step back. As I write these words, I think we're back a step, maybe even two.[69] Nevertheless, the trajectory is evident. Evangelicalism is not white supremacy, and we're not moving from bad to worse.

BUTLER CAN TELL a story of evangelicals' moral degradation—even as she describes meaningful and growing evangelical opposition to racism—because the movement has always contained both.[70] Take the two most important evangelical revivalists of the eighteenth century, John Wesley and George Whitefield. Wesley was an abolitionist. Whitefield was a slave owner.[71]

The Whitefield part is discouraging, to put it mildly. As that *Christianity Today* book review asked, how can people who claim to follow Christ so blatantly deny the clear teachings of the gospel? How could Whitefield preach God's grace and the Sermon on the Mount and yet fail to see what a grotesque and obvious evil he'd endorsed? Considering this history, reading accounts of lynching and other terrors of slavery and Jim Crow, I understand Butler's instinct to say a little yeast has leavened the whole dough.

But there's more than one yeast here. There's the witness of Wesley too, and of other evangelicals who followed him over Whitefield, even when that meant going against the grain of their culture. White evangelicals in Georgia in the 1890s, for instance, generally weren't vocal opponents of lynching—to their shame. Yet in 1897, a newspaper in the state complained that multiple pastors in Atlanta had preached against lynching one Sunday, griping that they must "have run entirely out of gospel subjects to preach on."[72] On the contrary, it sounds like the gospel broke through.

"If you were to look at the United States in 1860, you would see that Southern white evangelicalism was overwhelmingly pro-slavery," observed historian Daniel K. Williams when I interviewed him. "But that's not *intrinsic* to evangelicalism," he continued. "It was intrinsic to *Southern evangelicalism at that moment.* I think that's undeniable. But if you were to look at Oberlin College in 1860, it would be very strongly anti-slavery *and* very strongly evangelical."[73]

Our failings on race are real and must not be minimized—but neither should they be overblown, presented as universal, intractable, and definitional when they are not.

ONE LAST THING on Butler. From the outset, she purports to be telling a hidden history, "the story evangelicals won't" tell. I was aware of much of this history before researching for this book, but as it happens, I came to *White Evangelical Racism* directly after reading the very evangelical historians Butler names and derides (Noll, Bebbington, Marsden, Kidd—you've seen their names in these pages).[74] And precisely because I'd just read their work, very little in her book was new to me. This history isn't hidden. Evangelical historians *are* telling it.

Suppose, however, that Butler is correct: that the history is hidden, that we are deliberately whitewashing our movement's past and declining to teach our kids about the rank racism some evangelicals have advanced. I'm sure there are evangelical histories of which that's true, and this is dishonest and wrongheaded.

But that kind of lie of omission is also a mark *against* Butler's accusation of rising white evangelical virulence. If we only tout evangelical abolitionists and civil rights activists and hide evangelical participation in slavery and Jim Crow, that's evidence that we understand the gravity of those evils. It's evidence of justified shame and an effort, though misguided in its execution, to put distance between evangelicalism and racism. It's evidence of a desire to leave that past behind.

WHETHER WE CAN get distance is a central concern for historian and author Jemar Tisby in *The Color of Compromise: The Truth About the American Church's Complicity in Racism.* Tisby's charge is more nuanced than Butler's. He speaks bluntly of evangelical hypocrisy, but he doesn't equate the movement with white supremacy, and he writes not to condemn, but to educate and reform.[75]

When he turns from past to future, though, Tisby's message is muddled. On the one hand, he offers hope and guidance. "Christians deliberately chose complicity with racism in the past, but the choice to confront racism remains a possibility today," he says. If "racism can be made, it can be unmade." That may be difficult, but we have ample theological resources and models in church history to press on to unity and justice in Christ.[76]

On the other hand, Tisby repeatedly suggests that reform isn't possible because racism "never goes away."[77] He repeats this refrain, usually without qualification, at least half a dozen times, as if racism were the sole sin undefeated by the cross of Christ. "History demonstrates that racism never goes away; it just adapts," he says in one spot.[78] In another, having surveyed four centuries of race relations in America, he muses that maybe "Christian complicity in racism has not changed much after all," even if "the characters and the specifics are new."[79]

The specifics, it seems to me, are pretty important. A century ago, white Southern Christians were publicly torturing black people to death with the full approval of their communities.[80] This history is recent enough that there are photos, some printed as souvenir postcards, full of white people grinning like they've thrown a birthday party, not desecrated a human being for whom Christ died. In one lynching story Tisby relates, a white mob burned a pregnant woman alive, cutting her baby out of her and crushing the infant's skull. The mother's "crime"? Objecting to the lynching of her husband. This happened around 1918.[81]

What about today? Tisby is right that evangelicals "remain divided along racial lines."[82] That's visible in my church's sanctuary every Sunday—and probably in yours. As the prophet Jeremiah put it, "The parents have eaten sour grapes, and the children's teeth are set on edge."[83]

Yet it's also true, as Tisby notes, that evangelical views and behaviors around race have shifted enormously in recent decades. Polling shows pastors overwhelmingly believe "every church should strive for racial diversity," and white evangelicals easily "agree that black people should be treated fairly and have all the civil rights other citizens have." So far from condoning murder, "calling someone the n-word or expressly excluding black people from groups or organizations . . . usually elicits swift and unequivocal condemnation."[84]

In God's mercy, it is not 1918 anymore, nor even 1968.

NEARING THE END of *The Color of Compromise,* Tisby adapts a biblical proverb to say a prophet "has no honor in his or her own time." It took white evangelicals decades after the assassination of Martin Luther King, Jr., "to recognize King's contribution to American democracy and biblical justice," Tisby writes. "Certainly, changing attitudes can be viewed as a form of progress, but it is also helpful to remember that such positive perspectives on the [civil rights] movement have not always been popular."[85]

That's a good reminder of regrettable continuity. But it's also good to acknowledge real change. We were very late to recognize that King was right and that civil rights could not wait—but we did get there.

I mentioned I've seen evangelicals shift on interracial marriage, and I've seen the shift on King, too. When I was a first or second grader in a Christian school, the one that had started as a segregation academy, I distinctly remember feeling confusion about King. Everything I'd been taught made him sound like a hero, yet I had a strong impression that I wasn't supposed to like him or be happy he had a federal holiday. I couldn't square it. I wasn't even sure what questions to raise.

Three decades later, my twins are first graders, and they have no such confusion. Their first January in their Christian school, they came home from the MLK Day lesson having absorbed a straightforward message: *MLK was good. He did the right thing. He was courageous. We are celebrating him. We should be like him.* I hadn't anticipated how great my relief at this would be.

The twins are getting the elementary school version of that lesson, of course. As they grow older, they'll be in for fuller stories and harder truths.

They'll learn of evangelical failures and hypocrisy on race, but they'll also learn of our repentance and reconciliation so far. They'll learn about Whitefield but also about Wesley. They'll learn that the Southern Baptist Convention split from its northern counterpart in an evil infatuation with slavery. But they'll also learn that in the mid-1950s, the SBC passed a resolution supporting desegregation—by a vote of 9,000 to 50.[86]

They'll learn of evangelicals like Billy Graham, who embodied the "white moderate" King decried in his "Letter from a Birmingham Jail": the man who "paternalistically believes he can set the timetable for another man's freedom; who lives by a mythical concept of time and who constantly advises the Negro to wait for a 'more convenient season.'"[87] As King penned those words in his cell, Graham was busy telling *The New York Times* that King "would be well-advised to 'put on the brakes a little bit,' that his timing was 'questionable,' and that blacks and whites alike would benefit from 'a period of quietness in which moderation prevails.'" Graham refused to join the March on Washington, where King gave his "I Have a Dream" speech, and he criticized ministers who made "the race issue their gospel."[88]

But they'll also learn that Billy Graham leveraged his fame against racism even before King came to prominence. "There is no scriptural basis for segregation," he told a Mississippi audience in 1952. "It may be there are places where such is desirable to both races, but certainly not in the church."[89]

In 1953, Graham personally took down ropes segregating seating for a revival he was holding in Tennessee. He began privately lobbying Southern governors to move away from segregation,[90] then fought them on it in public.[91] In 1954, when the Supreme Court in *Brown v. Board of Education* ordered public schools to integrate, Graham urged Christians to obey.[92] By 1957, he'd hosted King onstage in New York City,[93] brought a black pastor onto his preaching team, begun working with black churches, and started suggesting that desegregation law might be needed.[94] When the Birmingham church bombing happened in 1963, Graham led fundraising efforts to rebuild.[95] In 1965, he called his integration work in Alabama "the most strategic and most important" of his revivals.[96]

"We should not mistake Graham for a civil rights activist," the historian Thomas S. Kidd concludes, "but he did stake his considerable reputation on desegregation."[97] He shifted the boundaries of acceptable opinion in the white South. And later in his life, Graham regretted that he hadn't taken bolder action.

"Tragically, too often in the past evangelical Christians have turned a blind eye to racism or have been willing to stand aside while others take the lead in racial reconciliation, saying it was not our responsibility," he wrote at *Christianity Today* in 1993, adding, "I admit I share in that blame."[98] In 2005, Graham said, "I think I made a mistake when I didn't go to Selma" for King's march for voting rights. "I would like to have done more."[99]

With the benefit of half a century of hindsight, it's easy to say that Graham deserved to regret his moderation. King's Birmingham letter stings, and so it should.

But consider also: Graham was a powerful, conservative white man who'd been raised in an openly racist home in the segregated South of the 1920s.[100] By the time he backed integration, he risked a great deal to take that stand. This isn't an excuse. It's just a fact. When we look at Graham's life, there's continuity, but there's real change too. If we ask, *Compared to what?* it's beyond doubt that his evangelicalism pushed him away from racism, not toward it.

As with Trump, let me make two last points. The first is that individualism is a defining mindset in evangelicalism (especially for white evangelicals) for both good and ill.

At its best, this thinking undergirds the Bebbington quadrilateral emphases on conversion and activism: Every single person needs salvation. Every single person must "go, and sin no more."[101] Every single person is made in God's image and worthy of our love and service.

At its worst, this thinking undergirds a convenient double standard: quick and forceful political solutions for our own problems, but the slow work of sanctification for other people's woes. Pannell saw this in his day, and he sketched it in *My Friend, the Enemy*:

> I know that the same conservative brother who refuses to link my social needs with his preaching of the Gospel is the same man who lobbies against the Supreme Court, fluoride in the water, and pornographic literature. "Something," he declares, "must be done about creeping socialism. We must speak out against the Communist menace, and by all means we must support the Dirksen Amendment on prayer in the public schools."
>
> But mention the inhumanity of a society which with unbelievable indifference imprisons the "souls of black folks," and these crusaders begin mumbling about sin. All right. I'll play the game, my brother. Whose sin shall we talk about?[102]

There's one more manifestation of evangelical individualism I want to describe, though. It's not the best or the worst. It's a kind of hypocrisy, inverted.

Ordinarily we think of hypocrisy as saying something good and doing something bad, professing a noble principle but not living up to it. This is the other way around. It's bad words but good deeds, and I've run into it many times over. The common pattern is for evangelicals in a political frame of mind to speak harshly about some group (like immigrants, racial minorities, or LGBTQ people) but then, when faced with a living, breathing member of that group, to fall all over themselves to be gracious and helpful.

I'm not alone in seeing this. Writer and pastor Justin Giboney told me about "friends who had serious racial hangups—but would do anything for me."[103] Author Rachel Gilson in an interview described evangelicals being "catechized such that the cultural piece and the individual piece are disconnected in our brains." We feel intense responsibility to the person in front of us, she said, "but when we're not faced with individuals, we're thinking about cultural, tectonic movement," and we may struggle to connect the two.[104]

Sometimes that connection arrives too late to do any good. It did for many white evangelicals with civil rights. Or, in a 2019 episode of *This American Life,* a Trump-supporting Christian described her dismay at witnessing hardline immigration enforcement against families in her town. She'd supported mass deportation in the abstract but was horrified when she saw children crying as their parents were taken away.[105]

But sometimes, we get there. In 2016, a political scientist discovered that a ballot initiative that would bring universal preschool to poor, predominantly black neighborhoods of Cincinnati passed significantly because a conservative, predominantly white, evangelical megachurch backed it. The church had been working on racial reconciliation, and members tried to stick to that principle beyond the interpersonal level.[106]

And sometimes, with inverse hypocrisy, the deeds prove more meaningful than the words. Along the border in deep red West Texas, *Christianity Today* reported on a pastor who still likes Trump's immigration policies yet feeds and shelters illegal migrants. "God told me, 'I want you to be my hands. My feet,'" the pastor explained. "'I want you to love them. Embrace them.'" This pastor has no say over federal immigration enforcement. But he's undeniably helping immigrants in desperate need.[107]

Or when Hurricane Helene happened, my then colleague Daniel Silliman recalled, "I helped a freewill Baptist church that had been covered in sludge, and we just shoveled out river mud for a few days. There was some preaching, a little sermonette about how [the Federal Emergency Management Agency (FEMA)] was trying to shut us down, but Jesus wouldn't be stopped. But then FEMA came and went, and we just said, 'Thanks guys, appreciate it.'"[108]

Or in 2025, a U.S.-Israeli agency spent months trying to find a charity willing to get humanitarian aid into Gaza. The only organization willing to help was Samaritan's Purse, the massive evangelical relief charity led by Billy Graham's son Franklin.[109] In the Trump era, Franklin Graham has become widely known for his strident right-wing politics. But under his leadership, Samaritan's Purse is helping people abandoned by the world.

FORMER NPR JOURNALIST Ken Stern spent time in evangelical churches in the run-up to the 2016 election, and he saw inverse hypocrisy too. He came away wondering why, "if many evangelicals devote their lives to helping others, does that not translate into a political agenda? How is it that anger and aggression have become the public face of Christianity, while the many acts of kindness and charity, and the spirit informing those things, are kept under a bushel, largely out of public view?"[110]

Stern's not exaggerating about the charity. Evangelicals are routinely among the most generous people in America. We spend twelve times as much money on overseas missions and relief work as on politics.[111] Our "households top the chart in the average amount donated" and "the percentage of people donating," per research from 2024, and that's giving "not only to [our] churches, but also to religious and non-religious charities."[112] Regular churchgoers are also markedly more likely to volunteer,[113] and we're the religious group most likely to say "God instructs us to protect the poor."[114]

Unfortunately, Stern also isn't wrong about the reputation, and that brings me to my second point: What we do and say in the public square matters. *When* we do and say it matters. Public anger and inattention to injustice don't negate private charity, but they sure don't complement it. Inverse hypocrisy is better than harsh rhetoric alone, but it would be better still to match words to deeds.

"With the tongue we praise our Lord and Father, and with it we curse human beings, who have been made in God's likeness," says the epistle of James. "Out of the same mouth come praise and cursing. My brothers and sisters, this should not be."[115]

Timing is particularly important in matters of race. Were I reading a medieval history book that said some majority group went from horrific terrorism toward a minority group to uncontroversial intermarriage with them in less than a century, I think I'd be impressed with the speed. If they were Christians, I think I'd marvel at the quick moves of the Holy

Spirit in sluggish human hearts. Likewise, were I reading about recent evangelical change on race from a remove of five hundred years, I think I'd find our progress miraculous.

But of course, we aren't at that remove. Even as it's possible to "see the miraculous nature of this change," said Edward Gilbreath, *Christianity Today*'s first black editorial staffer, "surveying history at a remove is a luxury that the people most impacted by that history don't have." After all, he told me:

> There's a huge difference between observing the history from afar and actually living it. When the history has implications for how you're viewed and treated socially, economically, and even theologically by the majority culture, it carries a greater weight and urgency. It's hard to be a dispassionate observer when your safety, freedom, and very existence are linked to the struggle.[116]

"ONE OF THE Bible's dominant narrative themes," Alberta writes in *The Kingdom, the Power, and the Glory*, "is the admonition to resist idolatry at all costs. Jesus frames the decision in explicitly binary terms: We can serve and worship God or we can serve and worship the gods of this world."[117]

Alberta is correct that "too many American evangelicals have tried to do both," not only in contemporary politics but over centuries of racial inequality, oppression, and strife. We can always stand to be better conformed to Christ, better habituated to living in love with the *whole* church. This, Gilbreath said, "is at the heart of addressing the growing cynicism, grievance, and misunderstanding that we're experiencing today."[118]

The reason that idolatry narrative is so dominant in Scripture, though, is that it's a perennial human temptation—and one of the most tempting "gods of this world" is our selves.

"There's a really convenient judgmentalism that sometimes comes from anti-evangelical voices," said Wear, the former Obama staffer.[119] It's a superiority that screams evangelicalism's wrongs and frailties and whispers what it gets right. In much criticism of evangelicalism is an implicit contrast, an update to the Pharisee thanking God that he is "not like other people," like the sinful tax collector: *We critics aren't fundamentalist bigots. We cast good votes and will know on our deathbeds that we were on the right side of history.*[120]

That may be. As the tax collector prayed, God have mercy on us sinners. I don't want to say evangelicals were right when we were wrong.

But neither do I want to excuse the refusal to recognize evangelical repentance and growth in good works when it happens.[121] Repudiating evil never requires downplaying good, and giving grace is not going soft on sin.

Neither do I want to forget that the great bulk of ordinary evangelical life has nothing to do with politics. It's about family, work, charity, church.[122]

Neither do I want to discount the multiplicity of evangelical politics. It was the Bebbington emphasis on activism that drew some evangelicals to the cause of civil rights—*and* to vote for Donald Trump because of abortion and trans issues. And it was the Bebbington emphasis on conversion and its transformation of individual souls that led some evangelicals to reject political solutions to racism—*and* to oppose Trump for his bad character.

And neither do I want to concede the ahistorical and ridiculous claim that evangelicalism is the worst of this country and chiefly to be blamed for its political polarization and animosity. Insofar as the hypocrisy accusation lands, the response for evangelicals is *more evangelicalism.* More Bible. More discipleship. More prayer. More church.[123]

As *New York Times* columnist Ross Douthat presciently warned a decade ago, you don't want a post-religious right.[124] You don't want this large bloc of conservatively inclined Americans to be *less* interested in ethics and answerability to God. That will not make for better politics by any measure. It will not make for greater pursuit of racial justice.[125]

"To me, people are more than their votes. And as hard as it can be sometimes, they're more than their views on race," Giboney mused in our interview.[126] "When I look at evangelicals, I say, *Okay, look at the movement that they've made toward adopting other people's kids, toward charity. Look at their innovations within the church.* There's a value there. I don't think all is lost for evangelicalism, because there are people who are preaching the gospel. There are good things going on."

CHAPTER FOUR

IMPOSITION

Okay, evangelicals hold their beliefs imperfectly but sincerely. Still, evangelicals should keep those beliefs to themselves.

THE WATER OF the soaking pool I'd chosen at the Olympus Spa was pretty perfect: 104 degrees and gently bubbling with hot tub jets. It was delightful, but I was exhausted and jetlagged from a red-eye flight and in the heat of battle between two powerful instincts. One was to people-watch, as I would at any other pool or beach, leisurely taking in the scene. The other was to carefully, constantly avert my eyes—to study the tile floor and the potted plants and absolutely nothing else—because everyone around me was nude.

Olympus is a traditional Korean spa. In some spaces, like the tearoom, you wear a light cotton robe. But in the large central atrium, where patrons rotate between pools, sauna, steam room, and tables for skin treatments, nudity is compulsory.

And this isn't a discreet nudity. There is *zero* privacy. You can't leave your towel by the side of the pool, then grab it on the way out. The rules are: Stow your robe and towel in a cubby, wash at an open shower station meant for twenty, then go for a soak with five or ten or forty other people.

If you're signed up for a Korean skin scrub, it's a full-body affair, also nude and out in the open. There's no tastefully positioned sheet like in a Western-style massage, no keeping on your underwear. My table was in direct sight of all the pools and about three feet from other patrons getting scrubbed on either side of me. My scrub technician was friendly, businesslike, and possessed of not a single qualm about scrubbing me *all* over.

Now, I should mention that my spa admission and scrub were free. When Sun Lee, the spa's owner, offered this experience while we were scheduling an interview, I thought about declining on grounds of journalistic ethics: Did it count as a gift? Usually, it's not appropriate for journalists to accept things from our sources. On the other hand, I couldn't tour the spa any other way; it'd be very weird to go have a look-see in street clothes.

I took Lee's point that visiting the spa would inform my research, but what ultimately convinced me to accept his offer was that it wasn't a gift I sought or—and I cannot emphasize this enough—would ever seek. As anyone who knows me can tell you, I'm a huge prude. I shudder at a regular locker room, let alone something like this.

What got me into Olympus was a commitment to thorough journalism. But what kept me there was the fact that *every* person I saw in the spa rooms, cleaning staff and scrub techs and customers alike, was female.

THAT'S JUST WHAT the state of Washington doesn't want. Olympus Spa is located in a northern suburb of Seattle, and it's embroiled in a multi-year court case over whether it can refuse to admit transgender-identifying males who haven't medically transitioned.

To be blunt, the spa staff can't discriminate among patrons with female genitalia. If a male has surgically transitioned, it may not be possible to tell the customer is trans, and it's not realistic for the front desk staff to deny admission based on looks or vibes or a lower voice. (Washington lets residents change their sex designation on state-issued IDs, like driver's licenses, so there's no reliable record for Olympus staff to check.)[1] But that arrangement isn't enough for Washington. State law says public accommodations can't discriminate on the basis of "sexual orientation," and it defines that category to include "gender identity, self-image, appearance, behavior, or expression."[2]

That is: If a male identifies as a woman, even if he has a fully intact and functional penis and testicles, Washington State says Olympus Spa must admit him. They must let him join the group showers. They must invite him to wander around the atrium, mingling with nude women and girls as young as thirteen. If he books a skin treatment, they must require one of their scrub techs to scrub him *all* over.

This is deranged. I thought it was deranged before I visited the spa, and I find it even more deranged after. Lee was right: The experience *did* inform my research. There is no world in which you can have a penis swinging around in that pool room. It is a vulnerable, intimate, *definitionally* female place, and you don't need to be a prude like me to see that. Letting males in there would be bad enough for the patrons. For the scrub techs, it would border on sexual assault.

This strikes me as a conclusion that would be obvious to at least 80 percent of Americans, just as many as think trans-identifying males shouldn't be permitted to play women's sports.[3] The Washington State Human Rights Commission (HRC) disagrees. Olympus *must* admit intact males who identify as women, the HRC says. It's fighting Olympus in court—and the spa is losing.

For Lee and his family, who've run the spa for two generations, this is about more than Korean tradition. Lee is an evangelical whose business policies are grounded in his faith. He wants the spa to stay female-only so his staff and customers can be comfortable, yes. But more than that, he wants to stick to biblical sexual ethics. Outside of marriage, Lee believes, men and women shouldn't be nude together. Keeping Olympus single-sex isn't just good for business. It's about following God's commands.

So when the HRC came after him, Lee told me, "It became clear that I had to choose: Am I going to proclaim my faith, or am I going to compromise?"[4]

THAT CHOICE IS unfortunately familiar. It's the natural result of the objection to evangelicalism I'm considering in this chapter. Unlike the first three, it's not concerned with the importance, merits, or consistency of our faith. It's about where and how we practice that faith, whether we can let it shape our lives.

Evangelicals can be religious, this perspective says, but keep it quiet. You can be personally pro-life, but as an employer, you must pay for insurance coverage for abortions. You can think gay marriage is wrong, but your bakery must still make a cake for a gay wedding. You can be privately convinced that people can't change sex, but shut up about it. Treat trans people exactly like the gender with which they identify. And do *not* proselytize. What you call "evangelism" is demeaning, judgmental, essentially harassment.

This perspective has become more prevalent of late, more clearly reflected in American policy and discourse. But Yale University legal scholar Stephen L. Carter saw it back in 1994, when he published a trenchant book called *The Culture of Disbelief: How American Law and Politics Trivialize Religious Devotion.*

"In our sensible zeal to keep religion from dominating our politics," Carter argues, "we have created a political and legal culture that presses the religiously faithful to be other than themselves, to act publicly, and sometimes privately as well, as though their faith does not matter to them."[5]

Carter opens the book with a litany of then recent examples, each more preposterous than the last: Hillary Clinton as first lady, under attack for wearing a cross necklace at official events. Televangelist Pat Robertson castigated as "a dangerous neanderthal" for holding the standard Christian belief that God can heal illness. A Supreme Court justice speaking about Jewish Sabbath observance as a matter of mere personal preference. A public school teacher ordered to hide his Bible in his classroom. A judge forcing a lawyer to wipe ashes off his forehead in court on Ash Wednesday.

The truth is, "we often ask our citizens to split their public and private selves, telling them in effect that it is fine to be religious in private, but there is something askew when those private beliefs become the basis for public action," Carter writes. Religion is diminished into "a quietly irrelevant moralizer," its public appearances treated as "presumptively wicked—indeed, as necessarily oppressive."[6]

And even then, in the early 1990s, Carter saw that this was particularly true of evangelicalism:

> Taking religion seriously is something that only those wild-eyed zealots do: Operation Rescue, blocking the entrances to abortion clinics . . . you know who we mean, those Christian fundamentalists . . . the evangelicals . . . the folks who want classroom prayer in public schools, but think that God doesn't hear the prayers of Jews . . . you know, those television preachers . . . those snake-charming faith healers . . . and the "scientific" creationists . . . *Southern Baptists,* for goodness sake! . . . There is a message in this miasma, and the message is that people who take their religion seriously, who rely on their understanding of God for motive force in their public and political personalities—well, they're scary people.[7]

And not only scary but manipulative and rude. In Christian Smith's *American Evangelicalism,* the 1998 book I referenced in chapter 1, survey participants described evangelicals as "those that go out and try to force their beliefs on others," judgy people who "stand out and yell at a crowd." Evangelicals whip up "unfounded paranoia" about loss of religious liberty when they come in conflict with gay rights, one man said. "I think that [evangelicals] are using those excuses as rationalizations to meet their self-serving needs."[8]

Two decades later, in *White Evangelical Racism,* Anthea Butler agrees. Evangelical talk about religious freedom, she says, is just a "means by which their beliefs could be imposed on the public," a "way to exclude LGBTQ persons from civil rights and to lobby for special status."[9]

In a 2015 book on hostility toward Christianity, sociologist George Yancey also documented these sentiments. His survey respondents described Christians as stupid, ignorant, intrusive, and frightening. "In a perfect world," one respondent said, "all Americans would be free to worship as they please, but that is to be confined to inside their homes and churches ONLY."[10] Even business owners like Lee couldn't bring their faith to work. "Keep your beliefs out of the public arena," said another. "Celebrate your religious choices in your unrestricted houses of worship."[11]

As Yancey observed, this conflict over the public expression of Christian belief intensified during the Obama administration. Then as now, the debate often concerned those two key issues for evangelical voters: abortion and ethics of sex and gender.[12]

These days, the latter makes more headlines. In the Obama era, abortion was the bigger fight, as the Affordable Care Act (Obamacare) required employers—including people who believe abortion is murder—to pay for abortion in insurance plans. "President Obama's administration supports religious values inside houses of worship," Yancey summarized, "but not when individuals want to live out those values in public." Religious expression is protected in the sanctuary but unfit to be seen in the marketplace.[13]

THAT PERSPECTIVE MAKES sense if you start with two wrongheaded assumptions. Carter described the first one: that "religion is like building model airplanes, just another hobby: something quiet, something private, something trivial."[14] In this thinking, church is a book club, albeit with an unusual number of rules. Attending Sunday services may be justly likened to going to brunch or visiting a theme park, as an infectious disease scholar told *The Washington Post* early in the COVID-19 pandemic.[15] Evangelism is rude just like any other intense and unwanted conversation.

Of course, this isn't how religion works. It's certainly not how Christianity works. Our faith can't be walled off in a "religious autonomous zone."[16] The apostle Paul does not urge us, "in view of God's mercy, to offer [our] bodies as a living sacrifice, holy and pleasing to God," whenever we happen to be at home.[17] The command is universal. We're Christians all the time, in all of life.

Evangelicals aren't alone in thinking this way. Soon after ascending to the papacy in 2025, Pope Leo preached that "our faith is authentic when it embraces our whole life, when it becomes a criterion for our decisions, when it makes us women and men committed to doing what is right and who take risks out of love, even as Jesus did."[18] If Sun Lee is serious about biblical sexual ethics, he has no choice but to limit his spa's admissions. He must obey God rather than the HRC.[19]

The second assumption is that a public square stripped of religion will be objective and neutral—that if faith is made private, we'll have purely secular conversations unburdened by the particular, exclusive, maybe even intolerant concerns of faith. In reality, the silencing of faith is not the summoning of objectivity. When we kick out religion, we don't get neutrality but a secular perspective that *pretends* to be no perspective at all.[20]

The spa case is a good example. The understanding of gender identity in Washington state law isn't neutral. It's not a view from nowhere.

Far from it: This is a hotly disputed perspective with implications reaching well beyond politics and skin scrubs. It gets to fundamental questions about human nature; about whether we have souls and whether those souls are somehow gendered; about what it means to be male or female, man or woman; about whether millennia of religious tradition (well beyond evangelicalism) is all oppressive bunk.

Perhaps it is—there are many honest, thoughtful people who've come to that conclusion. But there's a fair way to have that argument, and forcing religious people to hide their faith every time they step outside their homes and churches is not it.

HIDING IS WHAT Washington State would like Sun Lee to do. His legal troubles began in 2020, when the HRC received a complaint from Haven Wilvich, a male who identifies as a "nonbinary trans woman."[21] Wilvich contacted the spa to ask about admission, and the staff refused, citing the Olympus entry policy: "Biological women are welcome (and Post-operative Sex or Gender Confirmation Surgery MTF [male to female])."[22] Wilvich was not post-operative.

Lee doesn't remember Wilvich's inquiry, likely because this kind of question had become routine. Starting "maybe seven, eight years ago," he told me, Olympus began "getting some emails about whether a man can come in," including messages he believes were from LGBTQ activist groups trying to force a confrontation.

Until then, "we never thought that when we specify a woman, it had to be a *biological* woman," Lee explained, but "as we were getting all the emails, that's why we said, *Okay, we should say 'biological.'*" He didn't want to make a big deal of it and hoped that a small notice on the website—just enough to give the front desk something to cite—would be the end of the matter.[23]

It wasn't. "When we first got a letter from the Human Rights Commission, I didn't know what that was," Lee recalled. He thought it might be something to do with unemployment insurance. Instead, it accused the spa of violating state law and said Olympus must immediately begin accepting any patron who identified as a woman.

"Basically, it was saying that if I don't comply, then I'll be penalized financially—I don't know, monthly or yearly," Lee said. He reached an initial settlement with the commission in 2021 that required some of his staff to undergo inclusivity training. But then, on the advice of his attorney from the Pacific Justice Institute, a conservative legal nonprofit, Lee sued.[24]

THE OLYMPUS LAWSUIT didn't rely on a direct challenge to the law at issue, the Washington Law Against Discrimination (WLAD). That's wise, because the problem with WLAD's take on gender identity is about ethics, not language. The text seems straightforward, and (with legal expert Eugene Volokh) I suspect the HRC is correct to understand the statute as forcing Olympus to let trans-identified males with penises into its pools.[25] So Lee's lawsuit instead made a First Amendment argument regarding freedom of speech, association, and religious expression.

Lee lost. And then he lost again on appeal. In the most recent ruling when I interviewed him, a June 2025 decision from the U.S. Court of Appeals for the Ninth Circuit, all three constitutional arguments were rejected. (Lee lost once more in a subsequent appeal to the same court in the spring of 2026 and will likely seek a hearing at the Supreme Court next, but it's the 2025 ruling I'll discuss here.)[26]

The spa's lawsuit argued "that WLAD violates its right to free exercise by requiring the spa 'to renounce its [Christian] faith by its deeds.'" The Ninth Circuit opinion responded with the flimsiest possible understanding of faith:

> The First Amendment's Free Exercise Clause guarantees "the right to believe and profess whatever religious doctrine one desires," and proscribes "governmental regulation of religious *beliefs* as such." The government may not "compel affirmation of religious belief [or] punish the expression of religious doctrines." The spa is hard pressed to identify how WLAD regulates its beliefs. . . .
>
> [We] conclude that the spa's religious expression is only incidentally burdened. Though we recognize that the spa's desire to perform acts that contravene WLAD's mandate is motivated in part by religious belief, the HRC's action under WLAD does not prohibit the spa from expressing its religious beliefs.[27]

Got that? Lee's still free to *express* his beliefs. No one's saying he can't think—or say!—whatever he wants about God, the Bible, sex, and gender. He can do whatever he wants, provided it's in his own head or his own home or his own house of worship, provided it has no meaningful effect in his public life.

And, the court continued, this case isn't really about faith at all. WLAD doesn't target religion by name, and the HRC didn't talk about religion in its enforcement efforts against Olympus. Also, the spa isn't a church or Christian school, so it's not eligible for the kind of carve out, called a ministerial exception, those institutions are granted.[28]

Lee might think his beliefs are relevant—here, in his family business, precariously built by his immigrant parents with sweat, tears, and lots of prayer—but the Ninth Circuit says he's wrong. The HRC is threatening to take his money if he won't do as he's told, but that isn't a punishment for the expression of religious doctrine. His beliefs are unregulated! He's only being punished for *obeying* those beliefs, for acting like they're real and have moral weight and matter to the Creator of the universe.

He's only being punished for daring to live like an evangelical in Washington State.

PORTLAND, OREGON, AND Vancouver, Washington, are about two and a half hours south of Seattle, and I drove down there after I'd finished up my conversation with Lee at the spa. The next morning, I met with Lexi, the evangelical youth pastor I mentioned in chapter 2, at the home of Meagan and Kyle, a married couple with three kids. Meagan works part time at their church and co-owns a tattoo shop. Kyle is a tattoo artist himself and runs a shop where he employs several other artists, none of them Christians.

Lexi grew up in that area, but Meagan and Kyle are transplants, and all three expressed a wariness of talking about their faith with strangers. It's not shame, they told me, but a kind of social statistics: There's a very high chance—especially when anything to do with sex or gender is in the mix—that what they say will not be what their conversation partners hear.

Meagan is the most reticent of the three. "To be honest, I usually just avoid talking about faith at my shop," she said. "If anything ever comes up—about church or Christians, usually in a negative light—I'm just like, *I hope they don't ask me any questions,* which is probably terrible, but it feels so awkward. I don't want them to think that I am what they think of when they think about Christians: homophobic, racist, probably, Trump supporters and all that brings with it."

Kyle also described his evangelicalism as largely "incognito" at work. The other artists know he's a Christian, but mostly, he just tries to "be like Christ in the setting without saying, *I'm being like Christ.*"

As a youth pastor, Lexi doesn't have that option. Even so, when people in secular spaces ask where she works, "I get a pit in my stomach," she told me. "Not because I'm ashamed of what I do, but because I know what they're going to think of me. I know that they're thinking of something very incorrect," something less about Jesus than politics, and "really, really gnarly" politics at that.

In the context of relationships, Lexi said, or even conversations longer than a one-minute exchange with a barista, she tries to go deeper, to explain not just what she does and believes but why. "I'm also trying to not be as shy about it," she explained. "I mean, I talk to my friends in North Carolina, and they're like, *I've never been ashamed of my faith at all.* And I'm like, *Oh, wow.* It's not that I'm ashamed of it, but I've clearly got some kind of heart posture, some kind of embarrassment."

Lexi does outreach in the area's public schools, and she described the culture in the schools she visits as reliably skeptical—or outright hostile—toward Christianity. It's also unquestioningly embracing of any LGBTQ identity kids announce, even in the middle and elementary school years: "Truly anything goes, anything flies."

If students want to change their names and pronouns and

not tell their parents, the schools are fine with that. "It's common that I'll meet kids at school, then meet the parents later, and I'll say, *Oh, you're so-and-so's mom.* And they're like, *Who?*" Lexi said. "Yeah, it's common, very common."

Meagan and Kyle's kids go to a Christian school. She grew up in one and wanted the same experience for her children. Even so, Meagan said, her elder two are aware there's something unusual about them—that it's a bit odd to be an evangelical in Vancouver. The middle child asks about the meaning of pride flags and stories heard from public school friends. And in high school, Kyle noted, their eldest "is experiencing more relationships with kids who are dealing with deep depression and questions about sexual identity."

That kind of experience is nearly constant for many of the kids Lexi pastors. As I said in the introduction, *persecution* is too strong a word, including for what these students experience as evangelicals in a Portland or Vancouver public school. But the social challenges are real, and they feel overwhelming when you're ten or twelve or fifteen.

"At youth group, I talk a lot about being love and being light." Lexi continued:

> Jesus calls us to a higher standard, but we have to be lights in this world. I ask the students, *How can you be a light in your school?* They're like, *I don't want to do it.* They're scared. They're very timid, very embarrassed, because [LGBTQ activists and critics of Christianity among their classmates] are very vocal and very mean. My students are told that talking about Christianity is not what they're supposed to do.
>
> And when they hear that following Jesus is the harder road, they go, *I know you say it's good, but I don't see*

> *why that's worth it right now.* That's a very honest take on where my students are at because of how strong the social pressure is. Yeah, the social pressure is crazy.

That pressure has increased in Lexi's decade of ministry. School policies have changed too, in ways that Lexi feels make it more difficult for her to minister on campus. She never veered into complaint in our conversation, nor did Meagan or Kyle. They weren't whining or making excuses, just being matter-of-fact about the local culture.

Every now and then, Kyle said toward the end of our conversation, he and the other artists at his shop "get into these deep political or cultural conversations, and they love to present ideas that poke and prod, expecting me to fight them on it. And a lot of times, I agree with what they say. I'm like, *Oh yeah, absolutely*, and they're like, *What?*" Subverting mistaken expectations of Christians can itself be a stride forward.

"But then, once or twice a year, we enter into real conversation where they will ask a question, ask what I think," Kyle continued. "And then I kind of take a breath, and I'm like, *All right, here we go.* The room gets quiet. And it's the gospel."[29]

THE TENSION OVER LGBTQ issues I'm describing here isn't political—or rather, not straightforwardly so. It's not about evangelical participation in politics or governance by voting or lobbying or seeking public office. The kids in Lexi's youth group aren't trying to make a statement about gender transition. They're just trying to hew to ethics that were bog-standard across the political spectrum in the *very* recent past. They're trying to be faithful Christians without becoming total losers, a project anyone who remembers middle school can surely understand.

Even the Olympus Spa case isn't directly about politics. The spa operates in the metaphorical public square, but it's in the private sector. Lee never tried to get political power for himself. The HRC went to him, not vice versa. If anything, he came off in our interview as a man who'd like to be left alone.

Once he decided to push back on the HRC mandate, "the rest of it actually was God," Lee told me. "He helped us through it all—only thing I had to do was proclaiming." He sees that good has come of his court case and is amazed at how many people have rallied to his side. "So, I have no regrets in a sense," he said. Still he worries, especially for his kids: "I questioned God through prayer: *Why me?* We are just running this small business, and we wanted to just get along. Why do I have to be in the case where all the names publicly went out?"[30]

Many American evangelicals will never find themselves in Lee's predicament or close to it. Fairly few businesses so directly involve sexual ethics, and much of the country is friendlier to our faith than Portland, Vancouver, and Seattle. You're more likely to feel pressure to keep quiet if you're highly educated, live in a city, or work a white-collar job.[31]

Yet even outside those more intense situations, we all live and work in a country with ambient resentment toward public expressions of serious, life-directing religion, particularly ours. American norms on premarital sex, adultery, divorce, and gay marriage have shifted with remarkable speed.[32] On trans issues, the change has been even faster, if not quite as complete.

Sometimes, that shift holds even when it has harmful unintended consequences. In the state of California, for instance, per a 2023 law, you can no longer serve as a foster parent if you're not willing to provide an "affirming home" to a child with an LGBTQ identity.

That doesn't mean a specific LGBTQ child would be paired with a specific affirming family. It means *any* family on the roster, even those who will never be asked to host an LGBTQ child or those who work only with newborns, must preemptively sign on to "support and respect" LGBTQ identities. Any expression of unwillingness to affirm "must be considered conduct that poses a risk or threat"—a threat!—"to the health, safety, and well-being of a child."[33] This rules out most evangelical, Catholic, and other theologically conservative Christians. Not surprisingly, California is now dealing with a severe shortage of foster families.[34]

Is *that* a good balance of competing rights and beliefs? Is the idea that Christians who don't hold affirming theology are a "threat" to kids a *neutral* perspective? Is forcing traditional sexual ethics underground such an important cause that children must go homeless?

THERE ARE EXCEPTIONS, but evangelicals don't usually get into religious liberty fights because we're out looking for court battles. It's because we've stayed faithful to two thousand years of Christian tradition on these matters, and views about sex that were completely ordinary and mainstream suddenly became verboten.

The most influential evangelical theory of this situation comes from Aaron Renn, a writer who launched a thousand think pieces with a 2017 newsletter that became a 2022 essay that turned into a 2024 book, *Life in the Negative World.* Renn's idea is that modern American evangelicalism has existed in three eras, or "worlds."

The first era, from about 1964 to 1994, is what Renn calls "positive world." Not only was Christianity not weird, being Christian then would generally enhance your social status. Then came "neutral world," from 1994 to 2014. Being a Christian in public was still normal, but not necessarily a plus. Since 2014, Renn says, we've lived in "negative world," in which "society has an overall negative view of Christianity. Being known as a Christian is a social negative, particularly in the higher status domains of society. Christian morality is expressly repudiated and now seen as a threat to the public good."[35]

At book length, Renn has fine-tuned and nuanced his theory, accounting for cultural variations within the United States as well as how sub-Christian (especially racist) American culture in the positive world could be.[36] Still, given Carter's account—written in the positive world—and that sense that evangelicalism was "neglected, slighted, misrepresented" way back in the 1950s, I'm not sold on Renn's full model.

But negative world rings true, and Renn is correct that a society hostile to public Christianity will take an interest in evangelicals even when we want to be left alone. We're supposed to keep our faith private—and yet, Renn writes, "secular culture will not allow us to have a private faith. We will be confronted and asked to fall in line, and if we do not, we will face consequences."[37] That's what California is doing with foster parents, even revoking approval for non-affirming families who'd successfully cared for children in the past.[38]

Renn is also correct to think practically. I was impressed to find that his *Life in the Negative World* inverts the typical proportions of books of political or social commentary (including this one). Most books spend their first three-quarters explaining the problem, then pivot to a few ideas of what to do about it at the end. Renn's book is almost all solution-focused, and he's attentive to private-sector situations like that of Olympus Spa.

"Modern technological society provides many ways to impose indirect, subtle, and virtual pressures on people, ways that did not exist in the preindustrial society of the New Testament," he observes. The apostle "Paul was shipwrecked, stoned, beaten with rods, and imprisoned, but as far as we know, no one ever took away his ability to support himself as a tentmaker."[39]

RENN'S PRACTICAL IDEAS are a service to evangelicalism and other theologically conservative Christians. But he shouldn't have to offer them in the first place.

Let me reiterate that evangelicals aren't persecuted in America. On the contrary, we still enjoy exceptional religious liberty protections.[40] But those protections aren't always sufficient, as Lee's case shows, and they'll become toothless if Americans come to understand religion as something that properly exists only in the mind and the meetinghouse. Moreover, social hostility doesn't have to reach the level of persecution to be bad, and evangelicals shouldn't have to privatize our beliefs or abandon them to get along.

We also shouldn't have to stop evangelizing. I understand the resistance. I've seen evangelicals be obnoxious, off-putting, and downright offensive trying to tell people—especially Jewish people and other strangers running errands—about our faith. The single angriest online feedback I've ever received as a journalist came when I mildly suggested that evangelism, though often badly done, is not inherently immoral.[41]

The historian Molly Worthen made that same caveat when we spoke. "Evangelism is enormously heretical in our culture," she said, "and I get it. The whole premise of evangelism is, by the standards of multicultural modern pluralism, very offensive," Worthen went on. "At the same time, it's very straightforward: If you're a Christian, it is not complicated. There is no carve out for anybody, if Jesus is the Way."[42]

Christians like Worthen and me aren't the only ones to see it like this. Writing in *Time* in 2001, pundit Michael Kinsley, ethnically Jewish but religiously unaffiliated, marveled that warning people off a bad movie is considered helpful, but trying to spare them "an eternity of hellfire" is "widely considered a terrible insult." From a certain angle, he concluded, "it is insulting to Jews that Fundamentalist Christians don't try harder to convert us."[43]

The reason most of us don't, I expect, is twofold. One is that timidity Lexi's students have learned. We don't want to be obnoxious or unlikable, and we anticipate a negative reception, and we're not sure it's worth it.

The other reason is more directly remediable: We need to get our theological house in order, particularly regarding sexual ethics. We need to be clearer about what we believe, why we believe it, and what our beliefs require of *us.* Only then will we have the resources we need to live out faith in public well.[44]

Rachel Gilson, the author with whom I discussed inverse hypocrisy in chapter 3, is working on this. Gilson is attracted to women and married to a man, but she doesn't consider her testimony "a story of being gay and becoming straight."

"The truth is, even 10 years into my marriage, when I experience attraction to someone other than my spouse, that person is female," she wrote for *Christianity Today* in 2017. "Still, my marriage has been a place of joy and healing. When people ask me my orientation, my most honest answer is 'married'—with the same blessings and burdens of other married believers, and with the same source of hope and power, the Holy Spirit."[45]

Since that article, Gilson has published two books on Christian sexual ethics, one telling her story at greater length and the other addressed to parents. Her manner is calm and measured, and she's quietly resolute in her commitment to a traditional biblical understanding of God's will for human sexuality. But she's equally resolute about holding Christians to account for poor treatment of LGBTQ people, unseriousness about our own sexual sin, and shoddy theology built more on culture and instinct than Scripture.

Her experience at a conservative Baptist seminary "was that none of my colleagues has ever had even a *moment* of trouble with me being self-identifying same-sex attracted. Think of all the stories about homophobia or whatever—they were not bothered at all," Gilson told me.

But it's also true that "Christians have basically been jerks about this topic for a long time," she said. "We've done a poor job of teaching the Bible, and that has set up the perfect bed for affirming theology to take root." We may have been confident in our sexual ethics, but that confidence was unjustified. As soon as a serious challenge showed up—like a loved one coming out—it was obvious that "we've been under-resourced, theologically and biblically."

Maybe we could get away with that once, Gilson reasoned. Different times and places require attention to different aspects of our faith, and for most of the history of Christianity, there was no debate about same-sex relationships or gender transition. These recent shifts caught many Christians unawares.

That's understandable. The trouble is that the shifts also caught us too often speaking and acting in ways that undermined the credibility of our newly trumpeted sexual ethics. "We went from being the norm to outside the norm," Gilson said. "But the problem was we were the norm in the wrong way. We weren't *internally* the norm." On singleness, marriage, divorce, and more, "we were never as aligned as we thought we were. Marriage was male and female, but it was a very thin version of alignment."[46] We knew, at least generally, what the Bible had to say on these subjects and tried to follow it. But we hadn't really worked through the meaning of Christian sexual ethics for ourselves, nor had we learned to explain their logic persuasively and lovingly to those outside our faith.

EVANGELICALS HAVE WORK ahead of us on matters of sex and gender, theology and discipleship, and more. And, of course, we should be polite and considerate wherever we find ourselves. Yet our failures do not justify treating public religion as a sinister imposition. Following Jesus is not an at-home hobby. It is not like a light switch to be flipped on behind closed doors and shut off when we leave for work or school.

Sometimes faithfulness will mean Christians must give up opportunities open to others, particularly roles in government. If you believe God commands you to foreswear violence, you can't join the military. If you believe God is opposed to gay marriage, you can't be the town clerk in twenty-first-century America. Maybe you can successfully advocate for the law to change, but unless and until it happens, that's not your job.

Christians have recognized the necessity of this kind of

sacrifice since the earliest years of the church, when theologians like Tertullian argued that loyalty to Christ must take precedence over other allegiances. Christians who work for Caesar, Tertullian said, "are still the soldier and the servant of another; and if of two masters, of God and Caesar: but assuredly then not of Caesar, when you owe yourself to God, as having higher claims, I should think, even in matters in which both have an interest."[47]

But that's the government. In public life in the private sector—in civil society and the open market—evangelicals should be able to live and work according to our convictions. This is a reasonable expectation in a free society, where we all must learn to handle encounters with beliefs and practices different from our own.

As we finished up our conversation, I asked Sun Lee what would happen if he lost every appeal. While his case is being litigated, he's able to keep the spa admission policy as-is. But if he really, truly loses, what then?

"That's always back of my mind, what we need to do," he answered. "If we lose, then we may have to close. I don't think we can accept it."

We talked about moving out of state, but this isn't a laptop job that can be easily transplanted. His family has two spa locations and dozens of employees. What happens to their livelihoods?

"There's a lot of prayers, and it's very interesting times," Lee said. "At this point, I'm just leaving everything to God. I mean, once we close, we don't have anything."

Lee spoke quietly when he said that, as he had throughout our interview in the spa's small back office, crowded with cabinets and paperwork. He wasn't melodramatic. He wasn't raising undue alarm. But his situation *is* alarming. I've kept an eye on this case since 2023, and I still struggle to comprehend that it's happening in the United States.

What Lee and his family have been put through is indefensible. He wasn't hurting anyone. He isn't seeking attention or power. He isn't out imposing his faith on an unwilling public. He's simply trying to run his family business as is *required* by his understanding of God's will—a very defensible, ordinary, evangelical understanding that ought to be admissible in American public life.

Lee was right to choose to proclaim his faith rather than compromise. But the choice put before him was obscene.

CHAPTER FIVE

CONTROL

All right, evangelicals can believe in public. But they need to stop trying to control the rest of us.

THE PASTOR I was interviewing was a textbook case of white Christian nationalism—literally, provided your textbook uses the well-known rubric from Andrew L. Whitehead and Samuel L. Perry's *Taking America Back for God* and *The Flag and the Cross,* which Perry co-authored with Philip S. Gorski.

That rubric relies on asking people how much they agree with six statements:

1. "The federal government should declare the United States a Christian nation."
2. "The federal government should advocate Christian values."
3. "The federal government should enforce strict separation of church and state."
4. "The federal government should allow the display of religious symbols in public spaces."
5. "The success of the United States is part of God's plan."

6. "The federal government should allow prayer in public schools."[1]

Respondents indicate agreement or disagreement on a scale of one to four. And once you have the answers, the method is simple: You assign each answer a point value (also between one and four), then tally up the points.

The highest possible score is 24, and anything north of 18 makes you a Christian nationalist—an *Ambassador,* per the terminology in *Taking America Back for God.*[2] And though black Protestants tend to score high, Gorski and Perry say "whiteness" connects the political vision sketched by this rubric to Christian nationalism's "deep story" of an America founded on Christian values but corrupted by the "cultural degradation" of "'un-American' influences."[3]

The pastor I was talking to scored 19 when I gave him the survey, and that didn't surprise me given what he'd been saying—not to mention the concealed handgun he carried at his waist. "I love this country, and I understand even that is controversial for some people. But really, one of the biggest and most beautiful ideas in modern history is the idea of this country," he told me. When progressives "are trying to deconstruct this country, I get angry. Why are you guys doing this?"

He was particularly frustrated with Democrats like former President Barack Obama, whom the pastor saw as operating from an "ideology of almost asking for forgiveness to every single country" rather than standing up for America. He was wary of liberal moves against what he values—"which is family, the ability to have a nation"—and in favor of socialism.

And he worried about attempts to "destroy this country" by moving it away from its Christian heritage, hitting much of Gorski and Perry's "deep story" note for note. "The United

States," the pastor said, "was founded in Judeo-Christian values" and it "won't go well" to leave them behind.[4]

I HAVE TO fess up to one key detail I've left out of this account: This pastor isn't white. His name is Antonio, and he's an immigrant from Mexico and the husband of Jane, the evangelical Trump voter introduced in chapter 3.

Whitehead and Perry write that Christian nationalist Ambassadors like Antonio "are highly resistant to the idea that immigrants—even Christians who have been here for years—those who cannot speak English, and those without an American ancestor can be 'truly American.' [Immigrants] are indelibly 'them,' not 'us.' "[5]

But beyond being an immigrant himself, Antonio preaches in Spanish to a congregation of immigrants, many of whom aren't fluent in English and never will be. He helps them pursue legal status when possible and celebrates the opportunities and assimilation on offer to them in the United States.

Actually, here's another missing detail: His migration history is why Antonio loves America so much. "The biggest thing for me is that I'm an immigrant. I came here and I stay here because I love this country," he said. "It's not perfect, no, but I really believe that real freedom can be experienced in this country."

Antonio marvels that "even a person that doesn't have documents can start a business, can raise a family, can have a house, can have freedom." He's pretty sure that America's progressive critics have never traveled abroad to see real poverty, real corruption, or real socialism, like in the corrupt regimes many of his congregants have fled. American liberals "go to a beach, or they go to a resort," he said, and then imagine they know what life is like without the U.S. Constitution. He knows better.[6]

And, okay, just one more detail: Even though Antonio scored a 19 on the Christian nationalism scale, our interview and his engagement with the rubric both revealed nuanced thinking and a strong commitment to equal rights and liberties for people who aren't Christians.

"These questions are kind of tricky," he wrote to me after I sent him the six statements to consider. "It depends on the context and how you interpret what some of these words and concepts mean." On the one hand, Antonio believes the values the U.S. founders "drew upon were biblical, so if we deviate from them, we would be changing the direction of the principles our nation was built on." But on the other hand, "it's not about imposing Christianity as a religion."[7]

He'd emphasized that latter point at length when we talked. "The United States was founded in Judeo-Christian values," Antonio said, but that doesn't mean he wants theocracy, forcible conversion, or fewer rights for other Americans:

> I think there's virtue in Christianity—and in real Christianity there is going to be real forgiveness. It's going to be real tolerance. It's going to be real love. It is *real* Christianity. I understand that men in the name of Christianity have done mistakes. The Crusades. The Catholic church for years, even the Protestants in other parts of Europe. Even the Reformation, maybe, was embraced by the Germans to be used for a political movement. Whatever you want to find, you'll find it. But the *essence* of the gospel, the essence of God, is going to give us freedom. It's going to give us tolerance. It's going to give us acceptance. Not in

> the sense of everybody *has* to be Christian, you know? But real Christianity is going to give us real freedom.[8]

LIKE MANY EVANGELICALS, Antonio moves fluidly between God and government when he starts talking about America. The ideas, the impulses, the vocabularies all overlap. Even without prompting, his religion and politics naturally intertwine. I'm not sure he could explain how he votes without bringing up the Bible.

To hear many critics of evangelicalism tell it, that's a problem. Perhaps, they grant, evangelicals like Antonio—or Sun Lee—may be allowed to bring their faith into public life. Perhaps it's unfair to treat religion as a wholly private, housebound thing.

But for that allowance to work, these critics say, evangelicals need to keep quiet. Don't pursue power, and certainly not formal political power. That's liable to tip over into Christian nationalism, and in any case, religion-infused politics are inherently intolerant and antidemocratic. When evangelicals start politicking, it's because they want *control*. Dominance. Authority. However much they jabber on about heaven, their *real* ambitions have to do with earthly thrones.[9]

This became a common line of argument in the Trump era, but it's not novel.[10] Yale's Stephen L. Carter saw in the early 1990s that the "bedrock commitment to the authority of God as superior to the authority of the state" expressed by Martin Luther King, Jr., had in the span of just three decades become "suspect, the mark of the fanatic, especially when urged in service of positions often described as right-wing."[11]

In 2006, journalist Chris Hedges wrote in harsher terms.

"Most of America's fundamentalist and evangelical churches are led by pastors who peddle [a] non-reality-based belief system, one that embraces magic, the fiction of a 'Christian nation' in need of revitalization, and dark, terrifying apocalyptic visions," he alleged in *American Fascists.*[12] "Passivity in the face of the rise of the Christian right threatens the democratic state," Hedges warned, calling for conservative Christians to lose the First Amendment right to free speech—to preserve American liberty, you understand.[13]

A decade later, in the study I mentioned in chapter 4, George Yancey had survey respondents telling him that conservative Christianity ought to be excluded from American politics. "Religion in the political arena is dangerous to freedom and should be not allowed," said one person. "Even minor intrusions such as allowing religious groups to distribute public funds to the poor should not be allowed." Another likened the Christian right to "the Taliban in Afghanistan or the ayatollahs in Iran. We cannot allow them to get a solid foothold in our government."[14]

More recently, a *New York* magazine review panned Tim Alberta's *The Kingdom, the Power, and the Glory* for being insufficiently hard on evangelicals. "Joe Biden is the president, but in a real way, America is still under the evangelical boot," the reviewer declared. Even anti-Trump evangelicals are abortion "extremists" who "clin[g] to reactionary beliefs" on sex, and "the most vulnerable citizens of this country will never be safe" so long as evangelical beliefs have influence in American life.[15]

WHITEHEAD AND PERRY'S *Taking America Back for God* flirts with a similar view. It links evangelical political organizing to Christian nationalism, intimating some plot or menace. Evangelical lobbying groups like the Family Research Council "actively encourage Christians to work to ensure their worldview is represented in civil society," especially on social and sexual issues, Whitehead and Perry observe.[16]

Now, one could argue these groups are wrong on those issues. But surely what they're doing is unremarkable. Doesn't *every* activist group "work to ensure their worldview is represented in civil society"? Isn't that democracy? What's different when evangelicals do it?

Or, later in the book, Whitehead and Perry note—with, to my ear, a tone of approval—that the Freedom from Religion Foundation and other opponents of Christian nationalism believe "the particular interpretations of Christianity supported by Ambassadors and [Christian nationalist adjacent] Accommodators should have no place in structuring American civil life."[17]

But eight in ten evangelicals are classed as either Ambassadors or Accommodators per Whitehead and Perry's scoreboard—and I doubt the Freedom from Religion Foundation is taking pains to distinguish the other two.[18] In any case, we're talking about tens of millions of American voters. Should they really be run out of the public square? Should they have *no place* in structuring American civil life?

I understand the underlying concern here: My own faith has been indelibly shaped by the Anabaptist tradition, the strand of Protestantism most skeptical of politics and power. I believe American laws should be religiously neutral, never sectarian.[19] I value the Establishment Clause of the First Amendment just as much as the Free Exercise Clause.

And yet, for all that, it strikes me that this posture of suspicion toward evangelical politics is censorious and unjustified. It is not too much, even, to call it undemocratic. This is a vision of public life that preemptively marks evangelical conviction and reasoning out of bounds, then asks, scandalized, why evangelicals refuse to play by the rules. It draws the borders of public legitimacy so that evangelicals are ever on the outs.

Take advocacy. Whitehead and Perry look askance at the Family Research Council's activism, and Anthea Butler in *White Evangelical Racism* objects to the evangelical desire to "rule and reign"—that is, to see preferred candidates win elections and influence policy—as well as the formation of organizations to "openly lobby" for evangelical views.[20] (Would secret lobbying be better?)

But engaging in politics in a democratic system *always* means advocacy. It always means telling others what you suppose would be right and beneficial for the government to do. *Everyone* involved in American politics is, at some level, doing the same thing: seeking power to advance the moral and political vision they believe is good and prudent. If you're participating in democracy, of course you want to win. Of course you'll "openly lobby" for your ideas. Of course you'll seek influence. That's the whole concept.[21]

And evangelicals get to do this right along with everyone else—with the AARP and the ACLU, the NRA and NARAL, and many more besides—both by the rules of democracy and by the standards of evangelical conviction. "Clearly there are times when we should die to ourselves and endure injustice," as Yancey writes, "but the biblical interpretation that we never advocate for ourselves is incomplete. Paul did not hesitate to use his right as a Roman citizen to appeal his unjust treatment," and it's not necessarily power-madness for us to do the same.[22]

IS OUR POLITICAL engagement Christian nationalism, though? That's been the question of the hour for far too many hours, and often, *Christian nationalism* has been used as a lazy, fearmongering synonym for *politically conservative evangelicals doing something I don't like.*

But is it a fair and honest label for someone like Antonio? He's a textbook case of Christian nationalism, yet nothing like the boogeyman the phrase generally evokes.

In *Money, Lies, and God: Inside the Movement to Destroy American Democracy*, journalist Katherine Stewart explains Christian nationalism as a mindset of "catastrophism; a persecution complex; identitarianism; and an authoritarian reflex."[23] Like many evangelicals, Antonio *can* be a little too casual in talking about political opposition or social critique as persecution. But beyond that, he simply does not fit the bill. If Antonio and his score of 19 are the big threat to American democracy, you'll have to forgive me for concluding the threat's been overplayed.

To their credit, Perry, Whitehead, Gorski, and Stewart are trying to be more precise than most nationalism discourse. All four are careful to establish that, in Stewart's phrase, *evangelical* or even *white evangelical* and *Christian nationalist* "should no longer be regarded as interchangeable." Stewart takes care to note that what she calls Christian nationalism can be observed in many American demographics, including among people who make no claim to Christian faith.[24]

These are welcome gestures, but unfortunately, that standard of precision doesn't hold. Stewart writes so broadly of the nefarious designs of the religious right that in practice she sweeps just about every politically conservative Christian into a pile of horrors. The religious right's "ultimate goal is power," she charges, as if this were a revelation about a political movement.[25]

Opposing these factions, Stewart says in *The Power Worshippers: Inside the Dangerous Rise of Religious Nationalism,* amounts to "a political war over the future of democracy." That's because the religious right "does not seek to add another voice to America's pluralistic democracy," she asserts, "but to replace our foundational democratic principles and institutions with a state grounded on a particular version of Christianity, answering to what some adherents call a 'biblical worldview' that also happens to serve the interests of its plutocratic funders and allied political leaders."[26]

That all sounds troubling, but the specifics are questionable. In a chapter about "a new, global, religious, right-wing populist movement" that is "really about taking down modern democracy and replacing it with authoritarian, faith-based ethnic-states"—a "kind of global holy war"—Stewart introduces "the real backbone of this movement": a "network of churches that emphasize strict interpretations of the faith."[27]

Ominous! So who are we talking about here? Maybe Westboro Baptist? Some freak cult out in Wyoming?

Turns out, it's The Gospel Coalition, a theologically conservative but temperamentally and politically moderate evangelical network. On their homepage as I write these words are articles and podcasts about overcoming perfectionism, being gracious to your spouse, taking better care of the environment, attacking historic justifications for slavery, and encouraging pastors and laypeople to spend more time reading the Bible.[28] Such hard-liners, huh?

Also on Stewart's list: GAFCON, the Global Fellowship of Confessing Anglicans. As it happens, this is the larger Anglican network that includes my denomination, the Anglican Church in North America. It's a truly global denomination. The vast majority of our membership[29] and eleven out of twelve archbishops in our top governing body as of this writing hail from the Global South, especially Nigeria, Uganda, Kenya, Brazil, and other countries in Africa and Latin America.[30]

So how right-wing are these Anglicans? How backwards and controlling? How fixated on establishing faith-based ethnic-states?

So much that half the priests on staff at my church are women; that we have extensive ministries to refugees and other immigrants; that we have Democrats and Republicans happily coexisting in the pews; that we pray every week for the democratically elected leaders of our city, county, state, and nation regardless of their party affiliation. My family has had membership at this church for a few years now, but maybe I somehow missed all the stuff about the ethnostate?

Or maybe we're normal, and the Christian nationalism accusation has gotten out of hand. Maybe it's spread well beyond rightful and necessary condemnation of real authoritarianism and lawlessness to smear millions of ordinary Christians.

When she gets down to it, Stewart's concrete objections to The Gospel Coalition and GAFCON are that both hold traditional Christian ethics on LGBTQ issues and that TGC and some parts of GAFCON are complementarian, opposing women's ordination.[31] If *that's* what makes you a Christian nationalist doing a global holy war, I've got big news about 1,900 years of church history and an obscure little faction called the Catholic Church.

WHITEHEAD AND PERRY'S survey-based approach is more serious but also imprecise. Antonio wasn't wrong to describe those six statements as "kind of tricky."

Take the last one: "The federal government should allow prayer in public schools." This is likely intended to reference *Engel v. Vitale*, a landmark 1962 Supreme Court case that asked whether public schools could ask students to say a short prayer together on a voluntary basis. That is, an *official, school-sponsored* prayer. The court said no, and this is the case older generations tend to have in mind when they say liberals took God out of education.[32]

But the survey doesn't mention any of that. All it asks is whether prayer—private prayer? official prayer? Christian prayer? Muslim prayer? *any* prayer?—should be permitted in public schools.

If I take the statement at face value and think about private prayer by students, then I strongly agree. It would be an indefensible affront to religious liberty to say a fifth grader can't whisper grace over her lunch tray. But if I read the statement with *Engel v. Vitale* in mind, then I strongly disagree. It's not Washington's place to teach children about faith. It's not a public school teacher's place to ask other people's kids to say prayers from his religion.

So how should I answer this survey question? I have no idea, because I don't know what the statement means and, as a respondent, would have no way to find out.

Several other statements are nearly as vague. Does the federal government "allow[ing] the display of religious symbols in public spaces" mean a Christmas tree in the park? Blue and white lights at town hall for Hannukah? Usually that kind of thing is outside federal control. Or maybe it's not exclusively about government properties. Does "public" mean something more expansive? Is it about whether you can put a nativity scene in your store window? I don't know. Maybe! The survey doesn't say.

Or there's this one: "The federal government should advocate Christian values." That could be understood in downright theocratic terms. But as Whitehead and Perry document, the phrasing can also suggest *distance* from anything sectarian, as when some Americans want to see Christian values in government—but only because they see those values as a generic positive influence "which they agree can be found in other world religions, too," not because "these things are found in Christianity *alone*."[33] So how do I answer this? The equal worth of every human being is a Christian value. Justice and mercy are Christian values. I'm adamantly opposed to theocracy, but I do want the federal government to advocate for mercy, justice, and equality. I have no idea what I should say.

Any survey that requires this much guesswork is a garbage survey. In fairness to Whitehead and Perry, they didn't write these statements and so aren't responsible for the useless data such a survey will produce. But they did choose to use that data as the basis of their book—a book that, again, labels eight in ten American evangelicals as either Christian nationalist Ambassadors or Christian nationalist–adjacent Accommodators.

Given the basis on which it's made, is that a credible charge?

EVEN IF THEY didn't catch the problem with the survey statements, Whitehead and Perry ought to have clocked the glaring problem in the results: After evangelicals, the most Christian nationalist group is, implausibly, black Protestants. Just as many (about 40 percent) are Accommodators, and only slightly fewer (around 30 percent) are Ambassadors. In fact, when measured on race alone (as opposed to religion), black

Americans are—by a striking 15-point margin—more likely to be Ambassadors and Accommodators than anyone else.[34]

Which seems more likely:

A. The group whose history in our country is marked by unique, large-scale, state-enforced enslavement, abuse, and subjugation is eager for another round of authoritarian governance that tramples on the rights of minorities.
B. This is a garbage survey, and black respondents—and likely many other respondents too, including white evangelicals—scored as high as they did by guessing the more tolerant and generically positive meanings of those statements.[35]

Whitehead and Perry try to deal with the incongruity by writing that Christian nationalism has historically "shifted according to the cultural context that surrounds it." That's how white people used it "to both support and oppose slavery and Jim Crow laws," while black Americans used it "to oppose their unequal treatment in American society."[36] In the preface to an updated edition, the authors flag this section as insufficiently clear about how "Christian nationalism's pernicious effects are *racial* in their origin and character." The alarm they're raising is only about "*white* Christian nationalism," which is "associated with xenophobic and racist views."[37]

Xenophobia and racism *are* evil and alarming, but this post-hoc specification is just jimmying the data. The survey is poorly designed, and these results from black Protestants are the tell. It's well and good to talk about different historical contexts. But a "Christian nationalism" so malleable that it stretches from the Ku Klux Klan to Martin Luther King, Jr., is a concept broad enough to be useless.

WHITEHEAD AND PERRY have the right instinct when they cast about for a sympathetic explanation for black Americans' high scores. But they don't extend that sympathy to everyone else, nor do Gorski and Perry in *The Flag and the Cross.* One important example here will suffice: their handling of the violent pro-Trump riot at the Capitol on January 6, 2021.

This is an orienting event throughout the book, so it's vital for Gorski and Perry to show that the violence of that day "is not fringe"—that millions of white Christian nationalists supported the riot even if they didn't participate.

To establish this, Gorski and Perry share the results of a survey they conducted a month after the riot. They interpret the data as showing that white Christian nationalists believe this "violence was righteous and justified," that the rioters were "simply following the logic of the deep story: 'This is our country, not theirs. And we are at liberty to take it back by violence.'"

The survey results don't support this reading. Even at the maximum Christian nationalism score of 24, seven in ten white respondents supported prosecuting the rioters. This is less than the 95 percent or so who supported it at the low score, but still, a supermajority in favor of prosecution is remarkable. Even at that high end of the scale, only two in ten respondents said they "stand with" the rioters.

The more interesting results, however, come from the questions about who was responsible for the attack. These answers show a strong correlation with the Christian nationalism scores. Those on the high end were very unwilling to blame Trump and his spread of misinformation for the violence (less than 10 percent agreed) and very eager to blame Antifa agitators and Black Lives Matter activists (more than 90 percent agreed).[38]

Now, these respondents were dead wrong on the facts.[39] But their desire to disclaim the riot, to refuse to countenance the idea that their side, their leader, their people would trash the Capitol and attack police officers? That's a *good* thing. It's not evidence of an embrace of violence. It's evidence of rightful shame.

Even those most affiliated with Christian nationalism—and remember, this is affiliation measured by the same problematic survey as in the other book—want nothing to do with the Capitol riot. They're putting it on Antifa and BLM because they know the riot was wrong.

TALKING ABOUT THE Capitol riot is a good time to bring up one more piece of the conversation regarding evangelicals' supposed Christian nationalism: the New Apostolic Reformation (NAR) and its Seven Mountain Mandate (7MM).

These terms come out of charismatic and Pentecostal churches, which have a lot in common with median evangelicalism but also substantial differences. On the measure of *more or less* evangelical, most churches in this movement are somewhat *less*, even though there are many points of contact. A lot of contemporary evangelical worship music, for instance, comes from this tradition.

The differences between mainstream evangelicals and NAR types are apparent when you understand what kind of reformation the NAR groups believe is happening. They think

God has raised up a new generation of prophets, explains religion scholar Matthew D. Taylor in *The Violent Take It by Force: The Christian Movement That Is Threatening Our Democracy.* "They believe that Christians need to conquer the high places of influence in society and govern from the top down. Engaged in a cosmic spiritual war against the forces of darkness, they believe God has mandated them to use spiritual violence to defeat Satan and then build the kingdom of God on earth."[40]

The prophecy part is an obvious point of disparity. You don't hear Baptists or Anglicans talking about prophets like this. And though we also talk about spiritual warfare, it doesn't get nearly the same emphasis as in charismatic spaces.

That part about "the high places of influence" refers to the Seven Mountain Mandate. The idea is that there are seven spheres, or "mountains," of human culture: home; church; schools; the media; government and politics; arts, entertainment, and sports; and commerce, science, and technology. 7MM adherents believe Christians can serve God by doing good work in any sphere, on any "mountain."[41]

TAYLOR DESCRIBES ALL this as a conspiratorial menace. NAR Christians are going to "govern from the top down" in pursuit of "Christian supremacy."[42] Conquering the seven mountains "represents a deeply antidemocratic agenda," he alleges, calling the 7MM a "vision for world domination" and eliding the difference between spiritual and actual violence—that is, between energetic prayer and physically attacking another human being.[43]

The mountain language is only a few decades old, but this idea of different spheres of life has ample precedent in Christianity, including in markedly more staid branches like the

Reformed tradition.[44] Moreover, it's *good* for Christians to understand that they can serve God in any line of work, not just formally religious roles. And it's normal to want to pursue excellence and rise to the top of your industry. Trying to work hard and follow Jesus as a scientist or homemaker or film producer isn't Christian supremacy. It's standard-issue Protestantism with new branding.

Take this exhortation, for example, which mentions two of the mountains:

> You may be called to be a business executive. Study, get your management principles down and infiltrate the business world for Jesus. You may be called to be an athlete. Get out on the field and become the kind of athlete that can cause you to have an effective witness in the sports world; that is your mission field. If you are called to be a secretary, get it together, work your way up, become sharp secretaries to the top executives in this country. Secretaries influence executives. You can influence America from those offices. That's where the mission field is.[45]

Those aren't the words of an NAR prophet. They're the words of Tom Skinner, a black evangelist from Harlem who was invited to give the keynote address at Urbana '70, a conference of thousands of evangelical college students.[46]

To a predominantly white crowd, just two years after King's assassination, Skinner preached an uncompromising message on race in America. He presented Jesus as a liberator who demands far more of his followers than mental assent to a conveniently spiritual message. In addition to calling Christians to seek positions of influence in every societal sphere,

Skinner urged his audience to think in terms of spiritual warfare. If a policeman abuses him, Skinner said:

> I find out who is oppressing that policeman, then I must find out who is oppressing the man who is oppressing the policeman. I keep going until I get on a higher plane. Then I begin to understand what Paul means when he says, "We wrestle not against flesh and blood, but against principalities and powers, against the rulers of darkness, against spiritual wickedness in high places."
>
> The difficulty for us to understand as Christians is who really runs this world. . . . The kingdoms of this world belong to Satan, [so] what you and I as evangelical Christians must become is infiltrators, fifth columnists in Satan's world for the purpose of preaching liberation to an oppressed people.[47]

And as he concluded his sermon, Skinner thundered against any association of Jesus with nationalism or war:

> Just as the Indian Christians had to renounce the British Empire, I as a black Christian have to renounce Americanism. I have to renounce any attempt to wed Jesus Christ off to the American system. I disassociate myself from any argument that says a vote for America is a vote for God. I disassociate myself from any argument that says God is on our side. I disassociate myself from any argument which says that God sends troops to Asia, that God is a capitalist, that God is a militarist, that God is the worker behind our system.

> The thing you must recognize is that Jesus Christ is no more a capitalist than he is a socialist or a communist. He is no more a Democrat than he is a Republican. He is no more the president of the New York Stock Exchange than he is the head of the Socialist Party. He is neither of that. He is the Lord of heaven and earth. And if you are going to respond to Jesus Christ, you must respond to him as Lord.[48]

Accept the Christian supremacist framing and you might be able pass off those first two excerpts of Skinner's sermon as one more example of Christians grasping for power over our neighbors. But this last quotation—not to mention the rest of the address—shows the flaw in that framing: Nobody could imagine Tom Skinner a Christian nationalist.

This book is a defense of evangelicalism, and the NAR isn't typical of evangelicalism. In fact, *as an evangelical,* I think their understanding and practice of prophecy is wrong, and wrong in a way that's conducive to magnetic personalities amassing large followings with little accountability. But again, there are points of contact, and some elements of this movement that critics treat as threats, especially belief in the reality of spiritual evil and calls for Christians to use success in their work for God, are just regular Christianity with a layer of extra enthusiasm.

Urging Christians to seek influence for Christ through their careers is not malign. Talking of spiritual warfare is not a threat of physical violence. It's possible to believe these things and support Donald Trump. It's also possible to believe them as Tom Skinner. In neither case is that evidence of a "vision for world domination," except in the sense of the peaceable kingdom of God.[49]

WHEN EVANGELICALS PARTICIPATE in American politics, we tend to talk about our faith. These are the two contexts where we confront big ethical questions and ultimate ideas, so it makes sense that there'd be overlap. That's what happens when religious people participate in democracy—be they Christian, Jewish, Muslim, or part of any other religion—and religious speech was a normal, intelligible part of American politics until very recently. This kind of political engagement isn't necessarily—let alone usually—an authoritarian dynamic, and much of what gets called Christian nationalism doesn't deserve so exciting a name.

Moreover, Christian nationalism as measured by Whitehead, Perry, and Gorski is *declining.* This detail is briefly mentioned in *Taking America Back for God,* but, using the same survey data plus a fresh round from 2021, political scientist Ryan Burge gives a clearer picture.[50]

Two decades ago, more than half of Americans, 55 percent, believed "the government should advocate Christian values," Burge notes. "In 2021, that share had dropped to just 38 percent. That's substantial." The pattern holds with other statements from the survey and even if you filter out irreligious respondents. And crucially, evangelicals are no exception. Using the 24-point scale from *Taking America Back for God,* Burge found that evangelicals shifted from an average score of 15.9 in 2007 to 13.8 in 2021.[51]

I was surprised by those averages when I read them—a score of 13.8 would put you in the Accommodator section, but barely. It's middle-of-the-road, well below the high score of 24. I emailed Burge to ask about the math here: How could evangelicals' average score be so low if eight in ten evangelicals are Accommodators or Ambassadors, with scores of 12–17 or 18–24, respectively?

A small part of the answer is a difference of survey years. That eight in ten figure came from 2017's numbers, while the average of 13.9 came from 2021, in which 3 percent fewer evangelicals scored as Accommodators or Ambassadors. But 3 percent is nearly negligible.

The more important part of the answer, as Burge explained to me, is that evangelicals are scoring on the low ends of the Accommodator and Ambassador ranges. This average indicates they're more likely to score 12 than 17, or to score 18 rather than 24. That is, extremists—even by this muddled metric—are few.

As of 2021, the plurality of evangelicals are Accommodators, but that average score of 13.8 suggests they're clustered at the low end of the Accommodator group, far from the high-scoring Ambassadors. And even the Ambassadors are clumped toward the center, away from the very highest numbers in their range. Christian nationalism is on the retreat.[52] (Another round of this survey was completed in 2025 with three new statements added to the extant six in the Christian nationalism measure.[53] The full results, which could change or nuance the trajectory I'm seeing now, won't be public until 2027.)[54]

That said, you *can* find unambiguous Christian nationalism in America. Some online provocateurs now use the label about themselves. The slam-dunk example is Michael Flynn, a former general and U.S. national security adviser. Though he's Catholic, Flynn has argued that you "cannot preach the Bible without the United States Constitution. Period."[55] This is straightforwardly Christian nationalist. It's also heretical, stupid, and nowhere near the norm for evangelicals.

That reality is why, as church historian and sociologist

Grant Wacker said to me, "I'm very weary of the label *Christian nationalist.* If I may be sort of secular, I think it's bullshit."

"There are a lot of political nuts, but evangelicals are like everyone else, nuts in the same proportion," Wacker continued. "It's easy for the press to talk about Christian nationalism, because it's a way of dismissing these people, putting them down. It's a handy shorthand. It sounds scary. It's a headline-grabber, isn't it? So *Christian nationalist* I think is partly true, but partly an illusion."[56]

THE DAY AFTER I interviewed Antonio, I had a few hours to spare before my flight out of Dallas, and I knew exactly how to spend them: finding someone at a cowboy church.

I'd stumbled upon these churches a few months earlier. They're popping up elsewhere in the country, but the epicenter is Texas, particularly the Dallas area and westward to cities like Lubbock, Amarillo, and Midland. Cowboy churches aren't a denomination, and the concept is pretty much what it sounds like: church, with cowboy culture. Many have a rodeo arena right on church property. Some use the arena as their sanctuary.

My spare hours landed on a Monday, the worst possible day for it, because many pastors use Monday as a weekend. Still, I had to give it a shot, so I started south from my hotel, on a path that would take me from one cowboy church to another until I met someone or ran out of time.

The first one was a total bust. Completely empty, and no arena anyway. The second one was no longer a church at all. They'd moved to another building, and the new address was too far. I poked around on the map and found two more cowboy churches close to me and each other. They were my best shot before I had to get to the airport.

By the time I reached the third church, I was well out of the city, passing farms and a large animal vet. And as I turned into the lot, I knew I was in luck: There were three parked cars, and I could see the arena out back. Inside I met Paula, who co-pastors with her husband. Setting aside her lunch over my protests, she took a seat and told me about her church.

"We started in 2006," Paula said. "We were raised in Western culture—my father was a cattle buyer; my husband worked cattle—and there's a need for churches that allow people to come as they are. So many people don't feel comfortable in a traditional church because there's a lot of religion, a lot of rules," she continued. "But what people in the country are looking for is something that they can relate to, and that would be the cowboy churches."

Not everyone who attends works with livestock. But many do, and the arena is a big draw. "We do a lot of rodeos," Paula told me. "We do ranch rodeos for the adults and kids that can ride. We put on bull ridings." She showed me the sanctuary, decorated frontier style, with a log cabin backdrop and paintings of horses on the walls. Then we dodged fire ant hills walking over to the arena. The church keeps three horses, Paula's own, stabled onsite, plus a handful of cattle for roping. The arena is open air, but they hope to install a roof.

All this cowboy stuff was fascinating, and I'd never seen anything like it. As Paula and I talked, I realized that my church—with its formal liturgy and ornate sanctuary—is exactly the kind of religious experience her congregants want to avoid. The closest we get to a rodeo is a miniature donkey in the petting zoo at the annual church retreat. The cowboy church is so different from mine.

Yet the single strongest conclusion I drew from meeting Paula is that the cowboy church is also just like mine. They're evangelicals: They love Jesus. They study the Bible. They preach the gospel. They're helping people as they can.

"We have a homeless ministry," Paula told me, "where we go down to the streets of Dallas, and we love on and feed our homeless." It's on the church calendar for the first Saturday of every month.

"And we have a food pantry. We were just in here meeting to make sure we're ready to feed people now that the government is fixing to shut down." Outside, she showed me the dedicated pantry building, explaining that they'd ramp up distribution from once a month to twice a week while a then looming federal shutdown in the fall of 2025 kept SNAP payments (food stamps) from coming through. "We're the hands and feet of Jesus," Paula shrugged. "That's what we're supposed to do."

Over to the left of the food pantry was the pond, artificially symmetrical and likely dug for cattle. Three months prior, Paula said, they'd used it to baptize thirty-six people. Then another eight a month after that, then six more, many of them newly converted after showing up for rodeos.

"You can get a cowboy out here that won't go into church," Paula said. "You get 'em out here, and he's like, *Man, I really need to talk.* And he could receive Jesus right out here where he's comfortable. And that's the thing with us: We've got to reach 'em where they're comfortable, reach 'em where they're at." But really, she added, "we're just like any other church."

I WAS DETERMINED to meet someone at a cowboy congregation for two reasons. One was plain curiosity. The other was that cowboy churches seem all but designed for evangelicalism's critics: conservative, rural, predominantly white, prone to wearing Stetsons and talking about their Western heritage and decorating their sanctuaries with flags and Americana. Paula and I didn't talk politics much, but I could hazard a *very* confident guess on how she and her congregants vote. Also, rodeos!

If *Saturday Night Live* were updating the Church Lady to depict evangelicals not as prim moralists but as rowdy Christian nationalists, the character might well hail from a cowboy church. I could imagine Paula's community providing the opening anecdote in an alarmist magazine story about, say, America under the evangelical (cowboy) boot.

If *I* may be sort of secular, I think it's bullshit. Paula and her church and so many other American evangelicals aren't hurting anyone—quite the opposite. They're not a danger to freedom. They're not like the Taliban. They're not fascists peddling magic or dangerous populists trying to storm the Capitol and set up a faith-based ethnostate. They are fully capable of participating in American democracy, and they should not be ashamed to speak honestly of how their faith and politics connect.

As a matter of political strategy, sure, many evangelicals could be more sophisticated. Law cannot be religious in America, and religiously informed politics often need to be "translated" into something more widely intelligible and appealing. It's true that some evangelicals can't or won't translate, but their politics are not on that basis beyond the pale.

"Secularists are wrong when they ask believers to leave their religion at the door before entering into the public square," as then Senator Barack Obama told his party in 2006. "Frederick Douglass, Abraham Lincoln, William Jennings Bryan, Dorothy Day, Martin Luther King—indeed, the majority of great reformers in American history—were not only motivated by faith but repeatedly used religious language to argue for their cause. So to say that men and women should not inject their 'personal morality' into public policy debates is a practical absurdity."[57]

So it is—for all Americans, evangelicals included. When evangelicals talk about politics in religious terms, that's not evidence of a threat. It's not a sign of some ill-concealed longing for dominion. It's Christians taking serious things seriously. It's the democracy of a still-religious country at work.

CONCLUSION

YEARS HAD PASSED since I'd gone to a church like this. It was 9 A.M. on Sunday in Dallas, and my first stop was a nondenominational service northeast of downtown—the kind of contemporary evangelical outfit that gets people seated with a countdown video, starts the service by dropping the lights, and delivers communion in prepackaged, self-serve cups, the wafers sealed in tiny compartments above the juice.

I sometimes worshipped this way in high school and college, but recent years have found me in a very different (and less typical) strand of American evangelicalism. Think liturgy more than spontaneity, vestments instead of denim, and communion from a silver chalice rather than the disposable all-in-one. Our services start with a procession and a pealing bell. Almost never do we dim the lights.

Those are distinctions of substance as well as style, and I confess I'm not nostalgic for the more casual churches of my youth. I'm happy where I am. But as I stood in that service in Texas, at a church I'd never seen before and may never see again, what I noticed most was not where we diverged. It was how entirely at home I felt.

Often impatient with more expressive worship and unsentimental to a fault, I found myself crying through the songs, enamored of the baby dedication, delighted with the remarkably diverse congregation around me. Across the aisle, a father with a shotgun-wielding hunter monogrammed on his oxford. Next to me, a young Latino couple—engaged, I thought, or maybe freshly married. Down the row, an amen chorus of elderly black women. In the back, ushers efficiently finding seats for stragglers. Up front, nine (nine!) babies blessed in a single go.

Scripture was read. The gospel was preached. The announcement slides gave glimpses of a church committed to its city, enthusiastic in prayer, busy with generosity, and serious about discipleship in a way the earliest evangelicals would've recognized at once.

THAT AFTERNOON, I took an armchair in the nursing mothers' room with Brad and Angela, co-pastoring husband and wife. They told me about founding their church, how they were determined that it would be not only welcoming to the poor but *built* for them—to the point of asking well-off friends to wait to visit until after some congregational culture had been established. They now count thirty-five nations represented in their membership and are thrilled over the growth of a new ministry they've started in another impoverished Dallas neighborhood. We talked with that strange ease of evangelicals freshly acquainted, the somehow immediate intimacy born of shared understanding of what God is like and what he wants us to do.

Our conversation was not my final interview for this book, but it felt like a summation, a gathering together of many threads. Brad and Angela are evangelicals, church folk, Jesus people through and through. They have good news, and they can't help but share it.

Sure, they're interested in politics, she rather more than he. Angela loved the presentations of the gospel at the much-watched funeral of assassinated political activist Charlie Kirk, and she seemed baffled that this was derided as Christian nationalism. Brad reflexively dislikes it when people tear down America instead of trying to find and foster what's good. He tends to vote for Republicans because they're the "lesser of two evils" on abortion and LGBTQ issues.

That is to say, Brad and Angela are just what you'd expect a pair of middle-aged, middle-class white Texan evangelicals to be. Throw in a fog machine and they'd be just the kind of people with just the kind of church that evangelicalism's critics have in their sights.

And that's the problem. Brad and Angela—and ordinary evangelicals all over this country—are not the pantomime monster those critics describe. They're not the enemy within. They're not corrupting our country or polarizing a populace that would otherwise live in gentle, secular comity. It would be not merely false but slanderous to discount their beliefs as hollow, harmful, or hypocritical, to reduce their faith to a personal preference or a ploy for power unworthy of the public square.

"It's all about the kingdom of God and how our lives have been dramatically changed by the gospel of Jesus Christ," Angela told me. "And we're just here to see other people's lives dramatically changed by the power of the gospel of Jesus."[1]

SOMETIMES THEY DO talk politics from the pulpit, depending on what you count as politics. "I really felt led to do a series on race right before George Floyd was murdered. Our son's biracial, and we have a heart for diversity and different cultures," Brad said. "We'll address the issue—and any issue, including sexual issues—according to biblical morality and God's way and God's standard."

Lately, Brad's particularly concerned about the pornification of American culture, worried that Christians will be "cowardly" about speaking to God's view of sex and gender because we're scared of social censure or conflict at the office. But he's first and foremost a local pastor.

"I'm really careful, because we don't want to make it about politics," Brad explained. "And that's not out of fear," except the very pastoral and evangelical fear of alienating friends and neighbors from the gospel. People and relationships in Dallas take priority over distant national agendas and abstract social trends. Evangelical individualism can be misguided, but it can be deeply fruitful and faithful too.

"When Peter says honor the king, that would be Nero—who impaled Christians and lit them on fire to light his garden," Brad mused. "So you think about the dynamic of Jesus's day or the early church days, and you just don't see a lot about politics other than commands to pray for rulers that it might go well with you." As Christians, then, our first task is "honoring King Jesus and following his ways."[2]

IT'S TRUE THAT evangelicals haven't always done that. The movement is rife with flaws and failures, as any movement spanning centuries and continents and communities will be. Pick a vice and some evangelical or other will be guilty of it. Evangelicals have done and condoned and ignored terrible things, sometimes in characteristically evangelical ways. We haven't always loved God with our whole hearts or our neighbors as ourselves. We don't always look like Jesus.

All that is granted—evangelicals are sinners. The point of defending evangelicalism from its despisers, then, is not to exempt it from fair scrutiny. It's to clear out specious and spurious attacks so we can conserve what is valuable and make room for real repair.

Effective critique will be made from evangelicalism's own commitments and by its own people. We need less revulsion and ridicule from without, more reformation from within. Disdain does not bring renewal.

Reform is worth pursuing because evangelicalism is good. Its enthusiasm is a strength. Its core emphases—conversion, activism, Bible, cross—are right, needful, and complementary to the emphases of other branches of the church. Evangelicals do not need to jettison our tradition or dismantle our culture or denounce our forebears or leave our churches. We don't need to become Catholic or Orthodox, Episcopalian or exvangelical. We don't need to become jaded.

We can't be ignorant of our past or naïve about our present or complacent about our future. But neither should we be ashamed to be called evangelical.

I UNDERSTAND THAT may seem daunting. Just as I was beginning my research for this book, I read a book by the Anglican theologian J. I. Packer as part of a program at my church. Time and again, I was shocked to find him speaking positively about his evangelicalism. Where was his defensiveness, his caution, his reluctance to disclose?

Yet I was also shocked to find myself shocked. I work at an evangelical magazine. I graduated from evangelical schools. I go to an evangelical church. I'm already publicly evangelical. Why did I expect him to be defensive? Why did I have this vague sense that it was, perhaps, a little distasteful for Packer to be so happy about the whole thing?

I knew that working in political journalism had made me hyperaware of how poorly many people outside the church think of evangelicals. Even so, reading Packer showed me how accustomed I'd become to a measure of discomfort with my own movement. Not shame but, as Lexi the youth pastor said, certainly "some kind of heart posture." Some kind of worry that embracing evangelicalism without layer on layer of qualification would tarnish my name.

If that's a familiar instinct, let me share three analogies.

FIRST, EVANGELICALISM IS like Walmart. "When I go to a Whole Foods or a Trader Joe's," my former *Christianity Today* colleague Daniel Silliman told me, "part of the reason it feels special is because only fancy people go here." As a longtime Whole Foods fan, I was sorry to admit I knew exactly what that meant. Then he continued:

> But when you go shop at Walmart, it's like, *Oh man, there are some idiots and some crazy people here.* And evangelicalism is the Walmart of American Christianity. There *are* some horrible people in this space. But also, the equality of access and openness is important to me. I don't want to be in a movement that says you have to have a college education to really be a spiritual person, or you have to have essentially a certain level of cultural capital. I don't want to be in a place where I

> don't have to be troubled by these people. These are my people.[3]

They're my people too, and probably the saddest thing I've learned on the job at *Christianity Today* is how little we recognize that we belong to one another. Evangelicals are "neglected, slighted, misrepresented" *by evangelicals.* Many of the most vicious fights I've seen on social media were battles inside our ranks. Innocent differences, well-intended exhortations, simple mistakes—any and all of these, it seems, can be conscripted for our internecine spats.

At an event in 2025, a fellow evangelical writer made a comment about our assembled group being part of "the 19 percent." It took me a minute to grasp her meaning: evangelicals who were not the 81 percent, evangelicals whom she assumed had all voted against Donald Trump in 2016. She was thinking about *us* in opposition to *them.* I don't recall exactly what she said, but it was concerned with differentiation: How do we stay distinct from those people? How do we demonstrate that we're a different class of evangelical?

I'm sorry to admit I know exactly that impulse too. But it's an impulse I want to reject. I don't want to be in a place where I don't have to be troubled by these people. I don't want to go to a church of just the 19 percent. That vote isn't the measure of evangelicalism. Considered alone, those numbers conceal more than they reveal.

In the early twentieth century, while more sophisticated, mainline Christians "attacked structures that permitted poverty and need, it was Pentecostals, Nazarenes, and Fundamentalists that founded churches among the dirt-poor farmers of Oklahoma, the automobile workers of Detroit, and the millhands of Gastonia," observed historian Nathan O. Hatch in *The Democratization of American Christianity*. "Although these movements had their share of charlatans and autocrats, they were remarkably effective in forging moral communities among the poor, the sick, the ignorant, and the elderly."[4]

Those evangelicals fed, clothed, healed, educated, and evangelized. And they're—we're—still doing it today. Now as then, there are some charlatans and autocrats around. After all, everyone goes to Walmart. But that part is not the whole, and the whole does not warrant scorn.

SECOND, EVANGELICALISM IS like America. If I may paraphrase the movement's 1990s bête noire, Bill Clinton, speaking about the United States, "There is nothing wrong with evangelicalism that cannot be cured by what is right with evangelicalism."[5] For all that there is to critique, evangelicalism has much to offer its own. We have the resources we need.

Sure, there's detritus too. Lots of saccharine knickknacks and badly acted movies. I don't especially like contemporary Christian music and don't understand why so many do. But honestly, who cares? Tackiness is not a sin.

And the very scale that ensures we have our freaks and fringes—the Walmart of it all—brings assets and advantages too. We have great books and good thinkers, long traditions and venerable hymnody. We've held on to orthodoxies others have abandoned, adapted where others buckled, stayed fast where others went adrift. There are worse things to be than Bible thumpers.

We tend to be lightweights on church history, but that's remedied easily enough (and more echoes of the past linger among us than we often realize). In a chronically isolated and lonely age, evangelicals have remained a visible, tangible community. We still bring casseroles. We still lay on hands. We have the same Scripture as ever, the same Spirit as ever, and "Jesus Christ is the same yesterday and today and forever."[6] Evangelicalism has never been wrong about that.

The core claim of this movement is that "Christ Jesus came into the world to save sinners—of whom I am the worst."[7] It's that each of us—individually, personally—must be rescued by Christ, ransomed from captivity to sin, redeemed from the power of death and the devil by a God who loved us enough to die for us while we made ourselves his enemies.[8] And then each of us—individually, personally—must be sanctified, transformed and made ready to fill out faith with deeds, to follow Jesus wherever he leads.[9] At our best, not caring what the world makes of us, this is how evangelicals live.

Whatever else we do (and there *is* lots to do), we must start there. We must live up to the evangelical name, and any credible criticism will point us to this same reform: Be more serious. More studious of Scripture. More often in church. More faithful in prayer and diligent in service and capable of clear-eyed explanation for why we act and believe as we do. *Be more evangelical,* not less.

FINALLY, EVANGELICALISM IS like your mom. It's the community "to which I owe a filial debt," said Matthew Milliner, the Wheaton art professor, "because they nurtured my faith. When I look for scriptural precedent for staying evangelical, for staying in the church that I was reared in, I find: 'Honor your father and mother.' "[10]

Honor doesn't mean ignorance. It never requires turning a blind eye to wrongdoing or pretending not to see sin. I mean, you know your mom. You know what's wrong with her. You know how annoying she can be. You know all her irritating non sequiturs and unthinking clichés. You know precisely where her politics go haywire, the mistakes she keeps repeating, the ways that she tends to hurt people—the ways, no doubt, that she's hurt you.

But also, she's your mom. You know her kindness too. Her care and sacrifice. Everything she taught you, all the good you can't repay. You owe her a filial debt. You love her. You'll defend her from those who don't. You don't need to be in denial about your mom's foibles to tell a smart aleck on the playground that enough is enough: It's time to back off. And you don't need to be in denial about evangelicalism to come to its defense.

ACKNOWLEDGMENTS

I MENTIONED IN the conclusion that I tend to be unsentimental, and if anything, that's an understatement. I write for a living, but getting a nice note out of me is next to impossible. Sometimes, however, I must make an exception, and writing a book is one of those times. It's an enormous endeavor, and I am truly grateful for every bit of help I've received.

Thank you to my editor, Matthew Burdette, for urging me in this direction, and to my agent, Keely Boeving, for her advocacy and guidance along the way. Thank you to the rest of the team at Penguin Random House for your insight and support, and to Kevin Antlitz, Brad East, Austin Gravley, and Carrie McKean for early feedback on the project. Thank you to Alan Jacobs for a perfect foreword and incisive questions that sharpened my research.

Thank you to all my sources and interviewees, particularly Antonio and Meagan for their logistical help; Ryan Burge, Ed Gilbreath, and Daniel Silliman for their pointers and insights; and David Bebbington, George Marsden, and Mark Noll for their landmark labors in evangelical definition and history. Thank you to my colleagues at *Christianity Today*—especially Marvin Olasky, Joy Allmond, Kara Bettis Carvalho, Kate

Lucky, and Mia Staub—for your enthusiasm about this project and facilitation of my book leave.

Thank you to our church, its clergy, and our many wonderful friends there, especially our community group and the Mayhews and Van Patters.

Thank you to our nanny, Nicole, for her kind and reliable care of our children. Thank you to my mom and her husband, Frank, for all their varied help around our household. Thank you to our kids for their (sometime) patience with my reporting travel, and to my husband, Peter, an excellent father.

And thanks to the Lord, our heavenly Father, almighty and everlasting God, for a better and surer defense than I could ever provide.

NOTES

INTRODUCTION

1. "Why 'Christianity Today?'" October 15, 1956, *Christianity Today*, christianitytoday.com/1956/10/why-christianity-today.
2. Christian Smith, 1998, *American Evangelicalism: Embattled and Thriving*, University of Chicago Press, 179–87.
3. Jan G. Linn, 2017, *Evangelicalism and the Decline of American Politics*, Cascade Books, 2.
4. See, for example, Damon Linker, 2007, *The Theocons: Secular America Under Siege*, Doubleday; and Chris Hedges, 2008, *American Fascists: The Christian Right and the War on America*, Free Press.
5. Jennifer Bleyer, February 21, 2008, "Evangelicals like Us," *Tablet*, tabletmag.com/sections/arts-letters/articles/evangelicals-like-us.
6. Ross Douthat, 2012, *Bad Religion: How We Became a Nation of Heretics*, Free Press, 138.
7. Daniel K. Williams, August 7, 2024, "The Evangelical Diploma Divide," *Christianity Today*, christianitytoday.com/2024/08/evangelical-diploma-divide-election-politics-class-unity.
8. Bonnie Kristian, May 5, 2016, "The Idolatry of the Donald," *The American Conservative*, theamericanconservative.com/the-idolatry-of-the-donald.
9. Anthea Butler, 2024, *White Evangelical Racism: The Politics of Morality in America*, University of North Carolina Press, 139.
10. Carol Tucker, June 16, 1997, "The 1950s—Powerful Years for Religion," *USC Today*, today.usc.edu/the-1950s-powerful-years-for-religion.

11. H. L. Mencken, July 27, 1925, "Bryan," *The Baltimore Evening Sun,* faculty.etsu.edu/history/documents/menckenbryan.htm.
12. Matt Tebbe, September 19, 2024, "This is the heart of MAGA Christianity. 80%+ of white evangelicals support this," *X,* x.com/matttebbe/status/1836719233683648837.
13. John Pavlovitz, July 7, 2024, "The White Evangelical Church in America Has Failed America. It's Failed Jesus, Too," *The Beautiful Mess by John Pavlovitz,* johnpavlovitz.substack.com/p/the-white-evangelical-church-in-america.
14. Bonnie Kristian, October 1, 2018, "President Trump and the Evangelical Lust for Power," *The Week,* theweek.com/articles/797940/president-trump-evangelical-lust-power.
15. Ryan Burge, April 3, 2025, "Do church going people actually want their church to talk about the political divisions in the United States? Absolutely not. Just 14% of evangelicals want it to be discussed. 18% of mainline Protestants. 27% of Catholics. 29% of Latter-day Saints," *X,* x.com/ryanburge/status/1907781036802441247.
16. Ryan Burge, March 31, 2025, "I like this graph because it shows just how unique evangelicals are in American religion. When asked, 'how important are your views about religion to your identity and how you think of yourself?' 77% of evangelicals said 'very much' That's TWICE as high as any other group," *X,* x.com/ryanburge/status/1906686823616717124.
17. Bonnie Kristian, January 12, 2024, "The Trump Debate Is Dead," *Christianity Today,* christianitytoday.com/2024/01/trump-debate-is-dead-evangelicals.
18. John Fea, February 7, 2024, "What I Wish More People Knew About American Evangelicalism," *The Atlantic,* theatlantic.com/ideas/archive/2024/02/evangelicals-christianity-james-dobson/677362.
19. J. I. Packer, 2021, *The Heritage of Anglican Theology,* Crossway, 246.
20. Philippians 3:12.
21. Mark A. Noll, interview by Bonnie Kristian, August 21, 2025.
22. George M. Marsden, 2019, "The Evangelical Denomination," in *Evangelicals: Who They Have Been, Are Now, and Could Be,* ed. David W. Bebbington, George M. Marsden, and Mark A. Noll, Eerdmans, 24–25.
23. Darren Dochuk, 2019, "Revisiting Bebbington's Classic Rendering of Modern Evangelicalism at New Points of Departure," in *Evangeli-*

cals: Who They Have Been, Are Now, and Could Be, ed. David W. Bebbington, George M. Marsden, and Mark A. Noll, Eerdmans, 154.

24. Ryan Burge, March 31, 2025, "I like this graph." *Substack.*

25. Thomas S. Kidd, 2019, *Who Is an Evangelical? The History of a Movement in Crisis,* Yale University Press, 5: "More recent evangelicals (especially non-Pentecostals) have tended to speak about their 'personal relationship with Jesus,' terminology that became common among Protestants in the 1880s. In both cases, God's discernible presence is key. As anthropologist Tanya Luhrmann puts it, the 'feature that most deeply characterizes [evangelicals] is that the God they seek is more personally intimate, and more intimately experienced, than the God most Americans grew up with.' This intimacy with God has marked evangelicals since the 1700s."

26. Russell Moore, 2023, *Losing Our Religion: An Altar Call for Evangelical America,* Sentinel, 14.

27. Matthew 13:24–30, KJV: "Another parable put he forth unto them, saying, The kingdom of heaven is likened unto a man which sowed good seed in his field: But while men slept, his enemy came and sowed tares among the wheat, and went his way. But when the blade was sprung up, and brought forth fruit, then appeared the tares also. So the servants of the householder came and said unto him, Sir, didst not thou sow good seed in thy field? from whence then hath it tares? He said unto them, An enemy hath done this. The servants said unto him, Wilt thou then that we go and gather them up? But he said, Nay; lest while ye gather up the tares, ye root up also the wheat with them. Let both grow together until the harvest: and in the time of harvest I will say to the reapers, Gather ye together first the tares, and bind them in bundles to burn them: but gather the wheat into my barn."

28. Ross Douthat, October 9, 2025, "He Believes America Should Be a Theocracy. He Says His Influence Is Growing," *The New York Times,* nytimes.com/2025/10/09/opinion/doug-wilson-america-religion-theocracy.html.

29. Daniel Hummel, interview by Bonnie Kristian, September 9, 2025: "Even within the Doug Wilson world—and not just him—they don't see themselves as the mainstream. They see themselves on the margins of evangelicalism. They think 'Big Eva' is the problem. They think mainstream evangelicalism—the NAE and Tim Keller and Russell Moore—is the problem. They think they're the pure remnant."

30. Justin Taylor, February 21, 2018, "An Interview with Mark Noll and George Marsden on Billy Graham," *The Gospel Coalition,* thegospelcoalition.org/blogs/evangelical-history/interview-mark-noll-george-marsden-billy-graham.
31. Tim Perry, 2025, *When Politics Becomes Heresy: The Idol of Power and the Gospel of Christ,* Lexham, 7–8: "Evangelicals seem more eager than most Christians to write and read, sell and buy, more self-examinations, self-justifications, or self-flagellations than any other ecclesial community. As hard as it might be to believe both inside and outside the movement, thanks to near ubiquitous caricature of the unreflective evangelical in American popular culture, no external critic of evangelicalism can compete with us when it comes to criticizing our own. We are our own best and worst critics. I strongly suspect that this disposition toward self-criticism is written into our ecclesial DNA. Modern Anglo-American evangelicals have been trying to discern just what's wrong with us since the movement began; it is why the movement exists."
32. Marsden, "Evangelical Denomination," 22.
33. Brian C. Stiller, 2019, "To Be or Not to Be an Evangelical," in *Evangelicals: Who They Have Been, Are Now, and Could Be,* ed. David W. Bebbington, George M. Marsden, and Mark A. Noll, Eerdmans, 273: "A friend wrote, 'I no longer call myself an Evangelical.' Thoughtful, well informed but now I suspect feeling embarrassed, he has chosen to avoid a term used globally by hundreds of millions of Christians. For many within shouting distance of U.S. media circles and party politics, the word has become a banner of disrepute. 'Evangelical' is now a word disfigured by political pundits, muddied by protestors from the left and right, and brought into dishonor by self-proclaimed spokespeople who excuse inappropriate behavior and language as the necessary price for political power. The center has shifted, and many Evangelicals now wonder where they fit."
34. Scot McKnight, October 18, 2017, "Bury the Word 'Evangelical,'" *Jesus Creed,* patheos.com/blogs/jesuscreed/2017/10/16/burying-word-evangelical.
35. Kidd, *Who Is an Evangelical?,* 118.
36. Kidd, *Who Is an Evangelical?,* 2.
37. Pew Research Center, "2023–24 U.S. Religious Landscape Study Interactive Database: Evangelical Protestants," *Pew Research Center,*

pewresearch.org/religious-landscape-study/religious-tradition/evangelical-protestant.

38. Kidd, *Who Is an Evangelical?*, 52.
39. Pew Research Center, "2023–24 U.S. Religious Landscape Study Interactive Database."
40. Kidd, *Who Is an Evangelical?*, 2.
41. Ryan Burge, February 26, 2024, "The Rise of the Non-Christian Evangelical," *Graphs About Religion*, www.graphsaboutreligion.com/p/the-rise-of-the-non-christian-evangelical.
42. Timothy Larsen, 2007, "Defining and Locating Evangelicalism," in *The Cambridge Companion to Evangelical Theology*, ed. Timothy Larsen and Daniel J. Treier, Cambridge University Press, 1–12.
43. Ryan Burge, October 26, 2021, "Why 'Evangelical' Is Becoming Another Word for 'Republican,'" *The New York Times*, nytimes.com/2021/10/26/opinion/evangelical-republican.html.
44. Burge, "Rise of the Non-Christian Evangelical."
45. Ryan Burge, November 13, 2023, "Who Is Abandoning the Evangelical Label?" *Graphs About Religion*, www.graphsaboutreligion.com/p/who-is-abandoning-the-evangelical.
46. Pew Research Center, December 14, 2021, "About Three-in-Ten U.S. Adults Are Now Religiously Unaffiliated," *Pew Research Center*, pewresearch.org/religion/2021/12/14/about-three-in-ten-u-s-adults-are-now-religiously-unaffiliated.
47. Bob Smietana, November 19, 2015, "What Is an Evangelical? Four Questions Offer New Definition," *Christianity Today*, christianitytoday.com/2015/11/what-is-evangelical-new-definition-nae-lifeway-research.
48. Chris Butler, interview by Bonnie Kristian, September 9, 2025.
49. I am thinking of the Nicene Creed or, for non-creedal traditions, its contents.
50. David W. Bebbington, 2019, "The Nature of Evangelical Religion," in *Evangelicals: Who They Have Been, Are Now, and Could Be*, ed. David W. Bebbington, George M. Marsden, and Mark A. Noll, Eerdmans, 34.
51. David W. Bebbington, interview by Bonnie Kristian, September 16, 2025.
52. Aaron Earls, July 26, 2021, "Who Are 'Evangelicals' and Why Knowing That Matters for Your Church," *Lifeway Research*, research

.lifeway.com/2021/07/26/who-are-evangelicals-and-why-knowing-that-matters-for-your-church. It's also worth noting that only six in ten self-ID evangelicals (around 23 to 30 percent of U.S. adults, depending on the poll) affirm all four qualities of the quadrilateral.

53. Thomas S. Kidd, 2019, "Is the Term 'Evangelical' Redeemable?" in *Evangelicals: Who They Have Been, Are Now, and Could Be,* ed. David W. Bebbington, George M. Marsden, and Mark A. Noll, Eerdmans, 249.
54. Packer, *Heritage of Anglican Theology,* 23–24: "Evangelicals know and never forget that Christ loved the church and gave himself for it that he might sanctify and cleanse it and present to himself a glorious church not having a spot or wrinkle or any such thing (Eph. 5:25–27). . . . There has been so much [conscience-driven denominational fracture] in evangelical history that we often fail to fully recognize the characteristic church-centeredness of evangelicals. . . . We yield to no one in our enthusiasm and zeal for the glory of God in the church."
55. Ryan Burge, July 7, 2025, "How Distinctive Are Evangelicals, Really?" *Graphs About Religion,* www.graphsaboutreligion.com/p/how-distinctive-are-evangelicals: Self-ID evangelicals are more than twice as likely than other American Christians to attend church weekly, have a high view of biblical authority, and express no doubt about the reality of God. This is true across generations, and the last four decades have seen evangelical numbers on church attendance and biblical authority *rise,* even as both plummet in the broader population.
56. Kidd, *Who Is an Evangelical?,* 4.
57. Mark Hutchinson and John Wolffe, 2012, *A Short History of Global Evangelicalism,* Cambridge University Press, 242.
58. Meaghan Winter, July 26, 2021, "The Fastest-Growing Group of American Evangelicals," *The Atlantic,* theatlantic.com/culture/archive/2021/07/latinos-will-determine-future-american-evangelicalism/619551.
59. Kidd, *Who Is an Evangelical?,* 7: "Prosperity gospel teachers assert that the proper exercise of faith will inexorably lead to health, wealth, and 'victorious living.' Most outside observers lump in pastors such as Joel Osteen, Joyce Meyer, T. D. Jakes, and Paula White (who is the most visible of President Trump's religious advisors) with evangelicals. But there are good reasons not to concentrate on them in [considering evangelicalism]. Although many prosperity gospel

churches emerged from the Pentecostal tradition, their theology has so dramatically departed from historic Pentecostalism that many Pentecostal leaders distance themselves from the prosperity gospel preachers. In some cases, what historian Kate Bowler has called 'hard prosperity' teaching becomes unmoored not only from evangelical beliefs but from traditional Christian themes such as atonement for sin, the need for divine forgiveness, the reality of suffering, and the final importance of eternity rather than material success in this life. And while 'cessationist' evangelicals have serious misgivings about some Pentecostal practices (especially speaking in tongues), a much larger segment of evangelicals see the prosperity gospel as un-Christian charlatanism. You can find versions of 'soft prosperity' teachings in many evangelical and Pentecostal churches, but I have largely chosen to exclude hard-edged prosperity gospel churches from the story [of evangelicalism]."

60. Mark A. Noll, 2019, "One Word but Three Crises," in *Evangelicals: Who They Have Been, Are Now, and Could Be,* ed. David W. Bebbington, George M. Marsden, and Mark A. Noll, Eerdmans, 8–9: "It has long been obvious that America's black Protestant churches contain a higher percentage of members marked by the four Bebbington characteristics . . . than do white Protestant churches. Yet the American embrace of slavery, followed by culturally enforced segregation, means that whites and blacks who share these religious emphases have shared very little else. An evangelicalism that includes both blacks and whites makes sense from an angle focused on narrowly religious characteristics, but far less sense in the actual outworking of American history."
61. David W. Bebbington, interview by Bonnie Kristian, September 16, 2025.
62. Kidd, *Who Is an Evangelical?,* 9.
63. Marsden, "Evangelical Denomination," 17–18.
64. Noll, "One Word but Three Crises," 10.
65. David P. Gushee, 2020, *After Evangelicalism: The Path to a New Christianity,* Westminster John Knox Press, 19.
66. Douthat, *Bad Religion,* 33–34.
67. Martin E. Marty, 1996, *Modern American Religion, vol. 3, Under God, Indivisible, 1941–60,* University of Chicago Press, 103–4.
68. Carl F. H. Henry, 1947, *The Uneasy Conscience of Modern Fundamentalism,* Eerdmans, 2–3.

69. Douthat, *Bad Religion,* 35–36.
70. Marsden, "Evangelical Denomination," 17–19.
71. Molly Worthen, 2019, "Defining Evangelicalism: Questions That Complement the Quadrilateral," in *Evangelicals: Who They Have Been, Are Now, and Could Be,* ed. David W. Bebbington, George M. Marsden, and Mark A. Noll, Eerdmans, 171.
72. Pew Research Center, "2023–24 U.S. Religious Landscape Study Interactive Database."
73. Brad East, May 20, 2024, "The Loosening of American Evangelicalism," *Christianity Today,* christianitytoday.com/2024/05/loosening-of-american-evangelicalism-norms-taboos-liturgy.
74. Douthat, *Bad Religion,* 32.
75. Alan Noble, August 4, 2014, "The Evangelical Persecution Complex," *The Atlantic,* theatlantic.com/national/archive/2014/08/the-evangelical-persecution-complex/375506.
76. Scott Shackford, February 3, 2022, "U.K. Officials Want Even More Power to Punish You for Being Mean Online," *Reason,* reason.com/2022/02/03/u-k-officials-want-even-more-power-to-punish-you-for-being-mean-online/?nab=1.
77. Lora Korpar, March 30, 2022, "Lawmaker, Pastor Charged with Hate Speech for Quoting Bible Walk Free," *Newsweek,* newsweek.com/lawmaker-pastor-charged-hate-speech-quoting-bible-walk-free-1693385.
78. Megan Basham, 2024, *Shepherds for Sale: How Evangelical Leaders Traded the Truth for a Leftist Agenda,* Broadside Books, 96.
79. George Yancey and David A. Williamson, 2015, *So Many Christians, So Few Lions: Is There Christianophobia in the United States?,* Rowman & Littlefield, 10. See also 2–6.
80. Yancey and Williamson, *So Many Christians, So Few Lions,* 6, 9. See also 4–5, 8.
81. Yancey and Williamson, *So Many Christians, So Few Lions,* 10.
82. Bonnie Kristian, February 9, 2026, "The Popular Progressive Podcast Calling Evangelicals 'Cancer,'" *The Free Press,* thefp.com/p/the-popular-progressive-podcast-calling.
83. Pew Research Center, March 15, 2023, "Americans Feel More Positive Than Negative About Jews, Mainline Protestants, Catholics," *Pew Research Center,* pewresearch.org/religion/2023/03/15/americans

-feel-more-positive-than-negative-about-jews-mainline-protestants-catholics.

84. Daniel Silliman, interview by Bonnie Kristian, August 20, 2025.

CHAPTER ONE

1. Rogerio, interview by Bonnie Kristian, October 6, 2025.
2. 1 Peter 3:15.
3. June 21, 1971, "The Alternative Jesus: Psychedelic Christ," *Time*, time.com/archive/6839039/the-alternative-jesus-psychedelic-christ.
4. C. Smith, *American Evangelicalism*, 24. See also 22–23.
5. C. Smith, *American Evangelicalism*, 24–25.
6. C. Smith, *American Evangelicalism*, 25.
7. C. Smith, *American Evangelicalism*, 43.
8. C. Smith, *American Evangelicalism*, 43.
9. C. Smith, *American Evangelicalism*, 28, 45. See also 26–27, 29–30.
10. Kristin Kobes Du Mez, January 22, 2021, "Five Myths About Evangelicals," *The Washington Post*, washingtonpost.com/outlook/five-myths/five-myths-about-evangelicals/2021/01/22/9ff5cc44-5c29-11eb-8bcf-3877871c819d_story.html.
11. Shadi Hamid, June 17, 2024, "Trump Has Changed What It Means to Be Evangelical," *The Washington Post*, washingtonpost.com/opinions/2024/06/13/trump-evangelical-nonreligious.
12. Peter Wehner, March 3, 2024, "Where Did Evangelicals Go Wrong?" *The Atlantic*, theatlantic.com/ideas/archive/2024/03/evangelical-support-republican-trump/677610.
13. Ryan Burge, October 26, 2021, "Why 'Evangelical' Is Becoming Another Word for 'Republican,'" *The New York Times*, nytimes.com/2021/10/26/opinion/evangelical-republican.html.
14. Wehner, "Where Did Evangelicals Go Wrong?"
15. Noll, "One Word but Three Crises," 3.
16. Peter Wehner, December 9, 2017, "Why I Can No Longer Call Myself an Evangelical Republican," *The New York Times*, nytimes.com/2017/12/09/opinion/sunday/wehner-evangelical-republicans.html.
17. Scott Clement and Emily Guskin, December 12, 2017, "Exit Poll Results: How Different Groups Voted in Alabama," *The Washington Post*, washingtonpost.com/graphics/2017/politics/alabama-exit-polls.

18. Samuel L. Perry, 2024, *Religion for Realists: Why We All Need the Scientific Study of Religion,* Oxford University Press, xv.
19. Perry, *Religion for Realists,* 4. See also 45, 63, 66.
20. Perry, *Religion for Realists,* 12, 41.
21. Perry, *Religion for Realists,* 12, 41–42.
22. Jesse Smith, March 19, 2025, "REVIEW: The Scientific Study of Religion We Don't Need," *Current,* currentpub.com/2025/03/19/review-the-scientific-study-of-religion-we-dont-need: "This perspective offers a real and important insight, but Perry proceeds to overstate his 'belonging, not believing' thesis. It is one thing to challenge the notion that religious beliefs are formed purely through rational processes, or that once adopted, religious beliefs operate as 'unmoved movers' exerting direct control over our lives. But Perry goes further than this, effectively arguing that beliefs do not do *any* moving at all. . . . For Perry, it is identities all the way down."
23. Romans 7:15, 18–19, NIV.
24. Perry, *Religion for Realists,* 45, 46.
25. Perry, *Religion for Realists,* 46.
26. J. Smith, "REVIEW: The Scientific Study of Religion We Don't Need."
27. Perry, *Religion for Realists,* 47.
28. Perry, *Religion for Realists,* 102.
29. Perry, *Religion for Realists,* 46.
30. Perry, *Religion for Realists,* 38.
31. John Pavlovitz, 2025, *The Beautiful Mess by John Pavlovitz,* johnpavlovitz.substack.com.
32. Substack, October 8, 2025, "Bestsellers in Faith & Spirituality," *Substack,* substack.com/leaderboard/faith/paid.
33. John Pavlovitz, July 21, 2024, "Christian, Don't Feel Guilty for Leaving the Evangelical Church. Jesus Already Has," *The Beautiful Mess by John Pavlovitz,* johnpavlovitz.substack.com/p/christian-dont-feel-guilty-for-leaving.
34. John Pavlovitz, July 7, 2024, "The White Evangelical Church in America Has Failed America. It's Failed Jesus, Too," *The Beautiful Mess by John Pavlovitz,* johnpavlovitz.substack.com/p/the-white-evangelical-church-in-america.

35. Pew Research Center, "2023–24 U.S. Religious Landscape Study Interactive Database: Evangelical Protestants," *Pew Research Center,* pewresearch.org/religious-landscape-study/religious-tradition/evangelical-protestant; Pew Research Center, May 12, 2015, "America's Changing Religious Landscape," *Pew Research Center,* pewresearch.org/wp-content/uploads/sites/20/2015/05/RLS-08-26-full-report.pdf.
36. John Pavlovitz, September 20, 2025, " 'The Christian Left' Conversation with Thom Hartmann," *The Beautiful Mess by John Pavlovitz,* johnpavlovitz.substack.com/p/the-christian-left-conversation-with-887: Pavlovitz approvingly quotes his podcast guest, Thom Hartmann, speaking "about a group of Conservative religious people whose goal is 'not to save souls, not to awaken people, not to make the world a better place, not to fulfill the obligations that Jesus put upon Christians, but to expand their own wealth and power.' "
37. John Pavlovitz, January 21, 2025, "MAGA Christianity Is Anti-Jesus. Just Ask Jesus," *The Beautiful Mess by John Pavlovitz,* johnpavlovitz.substack.com/p/maga-christianity-is-anti-jesus-just.
38. John Pavlovitz, September 21, 2025, "Conservative White Christians Will Worship Anyone but Jesus," *The Beautiful Mess by John Pavlovitz,* johnpavlovitz.substack.com/p/conservative-white-christians-will.
39. John Pavlovitz, September 27, 2025, "What Exactly Do MAGAs Love, Anyway?" *The Beautiful Mess by John Pavlovitz,* johnpavlovitz.substack.com/p/what-exactly-do-magas-love-anyway.
40. John Pavlovitz, April 21, 2025, "An Open Letter to Hateful White Americans," *The Beautiful Mess by John Pavlovitz,* johnpavlovitz.substack.com/p/an-open-letter-to-hateful-white-americans.
41. Bonnie Kristian, May 2025, "The Christian Schools That Cried Wolf," *Christianity Today,* christianitytoday.com/2025/05/christian-schools-cried-wolf: I wrote about this at length.
42. Evangelical Christian Publishing Association, 2025, "ECPA Milestone Sales Award program," *Christian Book Expo,* christianbookexpo.com/salesawards.
43. *The State of Theology*, 2025, thestateoftheology.com.
44. Kate Shellnutt, October 2, 2025, "Survey: Evangelicals Contradict Their Own Convictions," *Christianity Today,* christianitytoday.com/2025/10/state-of-theology-evangelicals-confused-conflicted-belief.

45. Taylor, interview by Bonnie Kristian, August 29, 2025.
46. 1 Corinthians 15:14, 19, 30.

CHAPTER TWO

1. Matthew Milliner, June 11, 2025, "I Kissed Evangelical Elitism Goodbye," *Millinerd,* millinerd.substack.com/p/i-kissed-evangelical-elitism-goodbye.
2. Matthew Milliner, interview by Bonnie Kristian, August 19, 2025.
3. Kristin Kobes Du Mez, 2020, *Jesus and John Wayne: How White Evangelicals Corrupted a Faith and Fractured a Nation,* Liveright, 3.
4. Sarah Pulliam Bailey, July 16, 2021, "How a Book About Evangelicals, Trump and Militant Masculinity Became a Surprise Bestseller," *The Washington Post,* washingtonpost.com/religion/2021/07/16/jesus-and-john-wayne-evangelicals-surprise-bestseller.
5. Katie Reilly, September 10, 2016, "Read Hillary Clinton's 'Basket of Deplorables' Remarks About Donald Trump Supporters," *Time,* time.com/4486502/hillary-clinton-basket-of-deplorables-transcript.
6. Ed Pilkington, April 14, 2008, "Obama Angers Midwest Voters with Guns and Religion Remark," *The Guardian,* theguardian.com/world/2008/apr/14/barackobama.uselections2008.
7. Beth Allison Barr, 2025, *Becoming the Pastor's Wife: How Marriage Replaced Ordination as a Woman's Path to Ministry,* Brazos, 1–2: Complementarianism is "a patriarchal system born in white evangelicalism that uses the Bible to justify privileging male authority. Complementarians claim to support the spiritual equality of women and men even as they argue that God ordained a gender hierarchy and assigned a permanently subordinate role to women. Variation exists among complementarians (some enforcing it more strictly than others), but women in the complementarian church must yield at some level to masculine authority—which means complementarianism rejects the independent leadership of female pastors."
8. Tom Holland, 2019, *Dominion: How the Christian Revolution Remade the World,* Basic Books, 273–76.
9. Du Mez, *Jesus and John Wayne,* 301, 304.
10. Bailey, "How a Book About Evangelicals."
11. Du Mez, *Jesus and John Wayne,* 5.

12. Du Mez, *Jesus and John Wayne,* 8. See also 7, 9–10.
13. For example, Kristin Kobes Du Mez, September 21, 2025, "The Justice of Jesus," *Du Mez CONNECTIONS,* kristindumez.substack.com/p/the-justice-of-jesus.
14. Du Mez, *Jesus and John Wayne,* 8.
15. Bonnie Kristian, 2022, *Untrustworthy: The Knowledge Crisis Breaking Our Brains, Polluting Our Politics, and Corrupting Christian Community,* Brazos, 92.
16. Du Mez, *Jesus and John Wayne,* 4.
17. Du Mez, *Jesus and John Wayne,* 95: "Falwell had already imbibed anti-communism in his fundamentalist Baptist circles, but now the business interests of his town—and his new church—were directly linked to Cold War capitalism."
18. Du Mez, *Jesus and John Wayne,* 88–89: "Fundamentally, evangelical 'family values' entailed the reassertion of patriarchal authority. At its most basic level, family values politics was about sex and power."
19. Du Mez, *Jesus and John Wayne,* 90.
20. Du Mez, *Jesus and John Wayne,* 218, 235.
21. Du Mez, *Jesus and John Wayne,* 106.
22. Du Mez, *Jesus and John Wayne,* 233–34.
23. Du Mez, *Jesus and John Wayne,* 250.
24. Du Mez, *Jesus and John Wayne,* 97, 184, 185: "Christian citizens must rectify this situation. Lest Americans be misled by traditions of Christian pacifism, Falwell insisted that Christianity sanctioned military aggression."

    "It wasn't just the evangelical elite who supported a preemptive strike. In 2002, ordinary evangelical Christians were 'the biggest backers of Israel and Washington's planned war against Iraq': 69 percent of conservative Christians favored military action, a full 10 percentage points higher than the general population. In 2003, once the war commenced, 87 percent of white evangelical Christians supported Bush's decision to go to war, compared to 70 percent of Protestant mainliners and 59 percent of secular Americans."

    "In the early 2000s, white evangelicals were enthusiastic supporters of a military response to the September 11 attacks, but they weren't alone. In October 2001, eight in ten Americans supported a ground war in Afghanistan. The war in Iraq, however, was a harder sell."

25. Pew Research Center, March 19, 2003, "Different Faiths, Different Messages," *Pew Research Center,* pewresearch.org/politics/2003/03/19/different-faiths-different-messages.
26. Milliner, interview.
27. Du Mez, *Jesus and John Wayne,* 187.
28. Du Mez, *Jesus and John Wayne,* 188.
29. Jenny Jarvie and Stephanie Simon, December 7, 2006, "Manliness Is Next to Godliness," *Los Angeles Times,* latimes.com/archives/la-xpm-2006-dec-07-na-godmen7-story.html.
30. John Donvan, March 14, 2007, "Christian Men . . . Too Wimpy?" *ABC News,* abcnews.go.com/Nightline/story?id=2951718&page=1.
31. GodMen, 2007, "Events," *GodMen* (accessed via the Internet Archive), web.archive.org/web/20070318054117/http://www.godmen.org/events.htm.
32. Daniel Silliman, July/August 2021, "Promise Keepers Tried to End Racism 25 Years Ago. It Almost Worked," *Christianity Today,* christianitytoday.com/2021/06/promise-keepers-racial-reconciliation-reconsidered: "Promise Keepers was, after all, the largest movement in modern America pushing white people to reckon with racism and the most significant since the civil rights marches resulted in legislation, assassination, and riots. . . . Racial reconciliation was part of Promise Keepers from the start. Though the ministry is remembered more for promoting an ideal of Christian manhood and encouraging men to be the spiritual leaders in their homes, promise No. 6 (out of seven) was a commitment to reach beyond racial barriers."
33. Du Mez, *Jesus and John Wayne,* 203, 204.
34. Molly Worthen, April 2009, "The Controversialist," *Christianity Today,* christianitytoday.com/2009/04/controversialist.
35. CNN, August 8, 2025, "Pastor on a Crusade for Christian Nationalism," *The Situation Room,* transcripts.cnn.com/show/sitroom/date/2025-08-08/segment/02.
36. Douthat, "He Believes America Should Be a Theocracy."
37. Du Mez, *Jesus and John Wayne,* 94. See also 87.
38. Beth Allison Barr, 2021, *The Making of Biblical Womanhood: How the Subjugation of Women Became Gospel Truth,* Brazos, 190, 186.
39. Ryan Burge, June 13, 2023, "Should Women Preach? Huge Majorities of Evangelical Think They Should," *Graphs About Religion,* www

.graphsaboutreligion.com/p/should-women-preach-huge-majorities.

40. Barna, March 8, 2017, "What Americans Think About Women in Power," *Barna,* barna.com/research/americans-think-women-power: A 2016 survey with somewhat different phrasing found only four in ten evangelicals were comfortable with women in pastoral ministry.
41. Timothy Larsen, August 31, 2017, "Evangelicalism's Strong History of Women in Ministry," *Reformed Journal,* reformedjournal.com/2017/08/31/evangelicalisms-strong-history-women-ministry.
42. Silliman, interview.
43. Tim Larsen, interview by Bonnie Kristian, September 5, 2025.
44. Jim Davis, Michael Graham, and Ryan P. Burge, 2023, *The Great Dechurching: Who's Leaving, Why Are They Going, and What Will It Take to Bring Them Back?,* Zondervan Reflective, 113; James 4:17.
45. C. S. Lewis, 1952, *Mere Christianity,* MacMillan, 177–78.
46. Du Mez, *Jesus and John Wayne,* 167.
47. Kristin Kobes Du Mez, February 9, 2024, "About That Atlantic Piece," *Du Mez CONNECTIONS,* kristindumez.substack.com/p/about-that-atlantic-piece.
48. Du Mez, *Jesus and John Wayne,* 154.
49. Barr, *Making of Biblical Womanhood,* 24–25.
50. Gerald Hiestand, June 20, 2024, "Has Christianity Been Good for Women?" *Theopolis Institute,* theopolisinstitute.com/conversations/has-christianity-been-good-for-women.
51. Laura McClure, ed., 2008, *Sexuality and Gender in the Classical World: Readings and Sources,* Wiley, 148–49.
52. Holland, *Dominion,* 532, 494.
53. Barr, *Making of Biblical Womanhood,* 53–55, 61.
54. Barr, *Becoming the Pastor's Wife,* 186.
55. Barr, *Making of Biblical Womanhood,* 26, 28.
56. Du Mez, *Jesus and John Wayne,* 277.
57. Kathryn Joyce, May 5, 2014, "The Next Christian Sex-Abuse Scandal," *The American Prospect,* prospect.org/civil-rights/next-christian-sex-abuse-scandal.
58. Barr, *Becoming the Pastor's Wife,* 155.
59. Barr, *Becoming the Pastor's Wife,* 180.

60. Communications Staff, November 29, 2005, "Many Evangelicals Unwittingly Live According to Dictates of Feminism, Moore Tells ETS Audience," *The Southern Baptist Theological Seminary,* sbts.edu/news/many-evangelicals-unwittingly-live-according-to-dictates-of-feminism-moore-tells-ets-audience: "Evangelicals maintain headship in the sphere of ideas, but practical decisions are made in most evangelical homes through a process of negotiation, mutual submission, and consensus. That's what our forefathers would have called 'feminism'—and our foremothers, too."

61. James Davison Hunter, 1987, *Evangelicalism: The Coming Generation,* University of Chicago Press, 96–97, 104: "Though the husband and father has ultimate authority, that authority is qualified by an emphasis on sentiment. . . . In this sense, his authority becomes purely theoretical and abstract. The emphasis on the requirement of the husband to love his wife . . . is so prominent that the relationship remains hierarchical in principle only. . . . By redefining the husband's authority as an administrative technicality, the marriage relationship as a functional equality, and her nature as 'weaker vessel' in exclusively physiological terms, Evangelicals have been able to maintain the integrity of their commitment to biblical literalism while at the same time making the submission of women much less intellectually and emotionally objectionable."

62. Lyman Stone, May 24, 2022, "So with that in mind, let's turn to the horrible awful damning report @DavidAFrench mentions. The report identifies 409 SBC-affiliated *accused* abusers. It's unclear if that is 409 in churches *right now* or 409 *ever*. I'll assume *right now*. Also, that's *accused*," *X,* x.com/lymanstoneky/status/1529103471336636419.

63. Lyman Stone, May 24, 2022, "So 409 abusers. . . . out of how many? Well, right now the SBC has about 45,000 active churches. Assuming 2 personnel per church seems reasonable, so 90,000 people. Assume 75% male, and that 100% of abusers are male. So that's one accused abuser *per 165 SBC ministers*," *X,* x.com/lymanstoneky/status/1529104109437169668.

64. Lyman Stone, May 24, 2022, "So among SBC ministers it seems like the rate of sex abuse *reported the church* (which likely means *related to the church*) is about 1-in-165. For men on the whole, sex abuse *related to the justice system* is maybe 1-in-4 to 1-in-15.

These numbers are NOT strictly comparable," *X,* x.com/lyman stoneky/status/1529106193154998272.

65. Lyman Stone, May 24, 2022, "And they're also extremely crude ballpark estimates. But it's difficult to imagine a way to get the SBC stats above the general-male-population stats. This report *seems* to suggest the average SBC minister is a low sex abuse risk than the average American man?" *X,* x.com/lymanstoneky/status/15291064 74911387649.

66. Guidepost Solutions, May 15, 2022, "Report of the Independent Investigation: The Southern Baptist Convention Executive Committee's Response to Sexual Abuse Allegations and an Audit of the Procedures and Actions of the Credentials Committee," *Baptist Standard,* baptiststandard.com/wp-content/uploads/SBC-Guidepost -report.pdf, 5.

67. Molly Worthen, interview by Bonnie Kristian, September 5, 2025.

68. Lexi, Meagan, and Kyle, interview by Bonnie Kristian, October 24, 2025.

69. Tim Alberta, 2023, *The Kingdom, the Power, and the Glory: American Evangelicals in an Age of Extremism,* Harper, 229: In his book on evangelical politics, Tim Alberta exemplifies this kind of thinking: "The set-your-watch regularity of evangelical pastors being exposed for victimizing their church members is bad enough. What's worse is that Christianity has become institutionally desensitized to it. The odds are, some faith leader I respect and admire today will reveal themselves to be a fraud and a scoundrel tomorrow. And I won't be able to feign surprise or conjure righteous outrage. Because scandal is now baked into the evangelical experience in ways that distort our standards of leadership." But these are not the odds at all!

70. Larsen, interview.

71. Kristin Kobes Du Mez, June 23, 2025, "Jesus and John Wayne Turns 5!," *Du Mez CONNECTIONS,* kristindumez.substack.com/p /jesus-and-john-wayne-turns-5.

72. Alex Raycroft, October 16, 2020, "A Faith and Nation Fractured: Prof. Kristin Du Mez Reflects on Book Reception and Upcoming Elections," *Calvin University Chimes,* calvinchimes.org/2020/10/16/a -faith-and-nation-fractured-prof-kristin-du-mez-reflects-on-book -reception-and-upcoming-elections.

73. Kristin Kobes Du Mez, August 24, 2021, *WINNING and What It Cost Us with Kristin Kobes Du Mez (ep. 8),* In All Things Podcast, podcasts.apple.com/us/podcast/winning-and-what-it-cost-us-with-kristin-kobes-du-mez-ep-8/id1556164581?i=1000533029029.
74. Du Mez, *Jesus and John Wayne,* 3.

CHAPTER THREE

1. Antonio and Jane, interview by Bonnie Kristian, October 26, 2025.
2. For example: Bonnie Kristian, May 9, 2019, "Evangelical Trump Supporters, Please Just Be Honest," *The Week,* theweek.com/articles/840273/evangelical-trump-supporters-please-just-honest.
3. Moore, *Losing Our Religion,* 156–57: "The reason this identification [of evangelicalism with Trump] sticks with so many people is not because of the overwhelming majority of white evangelicals who voted for this particular candidate, but the seeming cognitive dissonance of choosing a promiscuous, profane, thrice-married casino magnate to restore morality to America. While some people outside the church might just shrug their shoulders at the perplexity of that, others will say that it proves what they've suspected all along—that evangelical Christians are hypocrites and interested not in morality but in political power and cultural dominance. That's not an unreasonable assumption. After all, for decades, they heard evangelical Christians say that 'character matters.' "
4. Du Mez, *Jesus and John Wayne,* 268.
5. Cheryl J. Sanders, October 30, 2020, "Were You There?" *Christianity Today,* christianitytoday.com/2020/10/were-you-there-2.
6. Aaron M. Renn, 2024, *Life in the Negative World: Confronting Challenges in an Anti-Christian Culture,* Zondervan Reflective, 192.
7. Alberta, *Kingdom, the Power, and the Glory,* 438.
8. James Dobson, September 1998, "Letter," *Dr. Dobson's Study,* ontology.buffalo.edu/smith/clinton/character.html.
9. Trip Gabriel and Michael Luo, June 25, 2016, "A Born-Again Donald Trump? Believe It, Evangelical Leader Says," *The New York Times,* nytimes.com/2016/06/26/us/politics/a-born-again-donald-trump-believe-it-evangelical-leader-says.html.
10. Steve Benen, June 30, 2016, "Dobson Walks Back Claims About Trump's Born-Again Conversion," *MSNBC,* msnbc.com/rachel

-maddow-show/dobson-walks-back-claims-about-trumps-born-again-conversion-msna871611.

11. Alberta, *Kingdom, the Power, and the Glory,* 113.
12. Bob Allen, March 16, 2016, "'Evangelical Elite' Just Doesn't Get It, Claims Pastor and Trump Supporter," *Baptist News Global,* baptistnews.com/article/evangelical-elite-just-doesnt-get-it-claims-pastor-and-trump-supporter.
13. Kidd, *Who Is an Evangelical?,* 122.
14. Michael S. Hamilton, 2019, "A Strange Love? Or: How White Evangelicals Learned to Stop Worrying and Love the Donald," in *Evangelicals: Who They Have Been, Are Now, and Could Be,* ed. David W. Bebbington, George M. Marsden, and Mark A. Noll, Eerdmans, 218–19.
15. Ryan Burge, interview by Bonnie Kristian, September 9, 2025.
16. Taylor, interview.
17. Hamid, "Trump Has Changed What It Means to Be Evangelical": It is easy to forget it now, but evangelicals initially were skeptical of Trump. During the 2016 Republican primaries, Sen. Ted Cruz (Tex.) was the preferred choice of churchgoing evangelicals, while Trump's strongest support came from evangelicals with lower levels of church attendance. During the primary campaign, when one influential Christian magazine surveyed 100 evangelical leaders, not a single one said they planned to vote for Trump."
18. Gregory A. Smith, July 21, 2016, "Churchgoing Republicans, Once Skeptical of Trump, Now Support Him," *Pew Research Center,* pewresearch.org/short-reads/2016/07/21/churchgoing-republicans-once-skeptical-of-trump-now-support-him.
19. Pew Research Center, August 8, 2016, "Many Americans Hear Politics from the Pulpit," *Pew Research Center,* pewresearch.org/wp-content/uploads/sites/20/2016/08/Politics-in-Churches-FULL-DRAFT-08-04-FOR-WEB.pdf.
20. Pew Research Center, July 8, 2021, "Pastors Often Discussed Election, Pandemic and Racism in Fall of 2020," *Pew Research Center,* pewresearch.org/wp-content/uploads/sites/20/2021/07/PDL_07.08.21.Sermons.pdf.
21. Pew Research Center, July 10, 2025, "In a 2022 Survey, Most Americans Opposed Churches Endorsing Political Candidates,"

Pew Research Center, pewresearch.org/short-reads/2025/07/10/in-a-2022-survey-most-americans-opposed-churches-endorsing-political-candidates.

22. Du Mez, *Jesus and John Wayne,* 266.
23. Alberta, *Kingdom, the Power, and the Glory,* 23.
24. Alberta, *Kingdom, the Power, and the Glory,* 258.
25. Alberta, *Kingdom, the Power, and the Glory,* 196: "Would a serious Christian see fit, I wondered, to condone this brutish behavior in any other area of life? Would they condone vicious ad hominem attacks if they were launched at the office? Would they condone the use of vulgarities and violent innuendo inside their home? Would they condone blatant abuses of power at their local school or nonprofit or church? If the answer is no, then why do they accept it in politics? Because politics is about the ends, not the means. Since the ends are about power—the power to legislate, the power to investigate, the power to accumulate more power—the means are inherently defensible, even if they are, by any other measure, utterly indefensible. This compartmentalization of standards is toxic to the credibility of the Christian witness. Many evangelicals have come to view politics the way a suburban husband views Las Vegas—a self-contained escape, a place where the rules and expectations of his everyday life do not apply. The problem is, what happens in politics doesn't stay in politics. Everyone can see what these folks are doing. Just as you might stop taking marital advice from your neighbor if you saw cell phone footage of him paying for prostitutes and cocaine in Vegas, you might stop taking spiritual guidance from your neighbor if you saw him chanting 'Hang Mike Pence!' at the Capitol Building. An extreme example? Perhaps. But bankruptcy—spiritual and otherwise—happens slowly and then all at once."
26. Alberta, *Kingdom, the Power, and the Glory,* 230.
27. Alberta, *Kingdom, the Power, and the Glory,* 228.
28. Alberta, *Kingdom, the Power, and the Glory,* 218–27.
29. Alberta, *Kingdom, the Power, and the Glory,* 352.
30. Alberta, *Kingdom, the Power, and the Glory,* 2.
31. Alberta, *Kingdom, the Power, and the Glory,* 444.
32. Alberta, *Kingdom, the Power, and the Glory,* 215.
33. Alberta, *Kingdom, the Power, and the Glory,* 43.
34. Alberta, *Kingdom, the Power, and the Glory,* 50.

35. Alberta, *Kingdom, the Power, and the Glory,* 444, 229.

36. George M. Marsden, 2019, "On Not Mistaking One Part for the Whole: The Future of American Evangelicalism in a Global Perspective," in *Evangelicals: Who They Have Been, Are Now, and Could Be,* ed. David W. Bebbington, George M. Marsden, and Mark A. Noll, Eerdmans, 285: "To reuse an old analogy that still seems helpful today, one way of understanding religious-cultural militancy in some older-stock white Protestant communities is to think of their experience as comparable in some ways to that of immigrants. Faced with the new cultural standards of modernity and inclusiveness shaping much of education and the mainstream media, they feel like strangers in their own land. Their taken-for-granted ideals, beliefs, and practices that they grew up with are now often ridiculed and even despised. Unlike actual immigrants, however, they share memories of having been the dominant group in the very national culture in which they are still living. So resisting assimilation to the new ways is not just a matter of separating from the cultural mainstream (although it may involve that), but it also involves a resolve to 'take back' their culture."

37. Alberta, *Kingdom, the Power, and the Glory,* 24–25.

38. Kristian, "The Trump Debate Is Dead": A portion of this section was originally published at *Christianity Today;* used with permission.

39. James 3:1.

40. Salena Zito and Brad Todd, 2018, *The Great Revolt: Inside the Populist Coalition Reshaping American Politics,* Crown Forum, 179–80: "'In the end that election came at a very consequential moment in the country; we have been heading in the wrong direction for years and a lot of us felt as though we had to do something to stop it,' Bayles says, belying a sense of urgency that ultimately got her past her hang-ups about Trump's character. The 'consequential moment' Bayles mentioned is made manifest by an increasing tension between a society bent on secular tolerance and restrictions on the exercise of religion. Two of the lasting outcroppings of upheaval during the Obama era were the fallouts from the Supreme Court decision decreeing gay marriage the law of the land, and the insistence—imposed by the party-line passage of the Affordable Care Act—that contraception and abortion services be not only available, but required as coverage in employee or government-provided insurance programs. . . . Those two cases, one in favor of religious liberty and

one spawning a ferocious corporate and media campaign against it, brought the threat to the First Amendment's free exercise of religion clause into full focus for many evangelicals, just in time for the run-up to the 2016 election. Then, on a mid-February Saturday in 2016, . . . Supreme Court justice Antonin Scalia was found dead on a hunting trip in Texas—removing from the court its most ardent and articulate defender of religious liberty."

41. John Warwick Montgomery, October 22, 1976, "Will an Evangelical President Usher in the Millennium?" *Christianity Today,* christianitytoday.com/1976/10/current-religious-thought-will-evangelical-president-usher.
42. Kristin Kobes Du Mez, January 23, 2021, "Kristin Kobes Du Mez: Five Myths About Evangelicals," *The Spokesman-Review,* spokesman.com/stories/2021/jan/23/kristin-kobes-du-mez-five-myths-about-evangelicals.
43. Kidd, *Who Is an Evangelical?,* 147.
44. Bryan McGraw, interview by Bonnie Kristian, September 4, 2025: "Think about on the more progressive side. You do lots of surveys, and climate change never rises to people's top four or five issues for a given election. But progressive politicians seemingly feel quite compelled to be on the left on any kind of energy or environmental protection issue. Presumably they know what their voters are interested in. Climate policy is just a given for these politicians, and only then do they move on to the other things that can differentiate them in the field."
45. Du Mez, *Jesus and John Wayne,* 251.
46. Gushee, *After Evangelicalism,* 142–43.
47. Michael Wear, interview by Bonnie Kristian, September 9, 2025.
48. Rogerio, interview.
49. Basham, *Shepherds for Sale*, 71.
50. R. C. Sproul, July 24, 2020, "May Christians Vote for a Presidential Candidate Who Denies the Trinity?" *Ligonier Ministries,* facebook.com/Ligonier/videos/may-christians-vote-for-a-presidential-candidate-who-denies-the-trinity/4206115496128310.
51. Glenn, interview by Bonnie Kristian, October 6, 2025.
52. *Christianity Today,* August 30, 1968, "Book Briefs: August 30, 1968," *Christianity Today,* christianitytoday.com/1968/08/books-in-review-295.

53. William E. Pannell, 1968, *My Friend, the Enemy,* Word Books, 6.
54. Pannell, *My Friend, the Enemy,* 121, 51.
55. *The Color of Compromise* is a good primer on this history, or for an even shorter introduction, see Rod Dreher, February 10, 2015, "When ISIS Ran the American South," *The American Conservative,* theamerican conservative.com/isis-american-south-lynching.
56. Pannell, *My Friend, the Enemy,* 62.
57. Pannell, *My Friend, the Enemy,* 104, 123.
58. Butler, *White Evangelical Racism,* ix.
59. Butler, *White Evangelical Racism,* 138.
60. Butler, *White Evangelical Racism,* 9, 138.
61. Butler, *White Evangelical Racism,* 4.
62. Butler, *White Evangelical Racism,* 4, 11.
63. Butler, *White Evangelical Racism,* 55.
64. Butler, *White Evangelical Racism,* 99.
65. Butler, *White Evangelical Racism,* 111.
66. Laurie Goodstein, November 6, 2008, "Obama Made Gains Among Younger Evangelical Voters, Data Show," *The New York Times,* nytimes.com/2008/11/07/us/politics/07religion.html.
67. Michael O. Emerson and Christian Smith, 2000, *Divided by Faith: Evangelical Religion and the Problem of Race in America,* Oxford University Press, 52.
68. Butler, *White Evangelical Racism,* xii, 86–88, 91–94.
69. Justin Giboney, January 17, 2025, "Racial Unity Is out of Style," *Christianity Today,* christianitytoday.com/2025/01/racial-unity-out-of-style-reconciliation-mlk.
70. Butler, *White Evangelical Racism,* 15, 9–10, 22: Butler acknowledges that "American evangelicals made important and substantial contributions to the abolitionist movement and to the education and uplift of African Americans during Reconstruction," that many "evangelicals were abolitionists, supported the poor, did mission work around the globe, and made a better world for everyone," that antislavery evangelicals in the run-up to the Civil War were serious enough about abolition to break apart their denominations.
71. Karen Swallow Prior, 2023, *The Evangelical Imagination: How Stories, Images & Metaphors Created a Culture in Crisis,* Brazos, 64.
72. Kidd, *Who Is an Evangelical?,* 66.

73. Daniel K. Williams, interview by Bonnie Kristian, August 28, 2025.
74. Butler, *White Evangelical Racism,* 4, 12.
75. Jemar Tisby, 2019, *The Color of Compromise: The Truth About the American Church's Complicity in Racism,* Zondervan Reflective, 14–15, 17, 31.
76. Tisby, *Color of Compromise,* 19, 39.
77. Tisby, *Color of Compromise,* 155. See also 19, 110, 154, 171, 191.
78. Tisby, *Color of Compromise,* 19.
79. Tisby, *Color of Compromise,* 191.
80. Kidd, *Who Is an Evangelical?,* 64.
81. Tisby, *Color of Compromise,* 191.
82. Tisby, *Color of Compromise,* 174.
83. Jeremiah 31:29.
84. Tisby, *Color of Compromise,* 174, 181.
85. Tisby, *Color of Compromise,* 150–51.
86. Benjamin Schwarz, September 2003, "New & Noteworthy: What to Read This Month," *The Atlantic,* theatlantic.com/magazine/archive/2003/11/new-noteworthy/376922.
87. Martin Luther King, Jr., April 16, 1963, "Letter from a Birmingham Jail," *African Studies Center—University of Pennsylvania,* www.africa.upenn.edu/Articles_Gen/Letter_Birmingham.html.
88. William Martin, 2018, *A Prophet with Honor: The Billy Graham Story,* Zondervan, 301–2.
89. Edward Gilbreath, October 1, 2000, "Billy Graham Had a Dream," *Christianity Today,* christianitytoday.com/1995/07/apostle-paul-and-his-times-history-in-making-billy.
90. John Blake, February 22, 2018, "Where Billy Graham 'Missed the Mark,'" *CNN,* cnn.com/2018/02/22/us/billy-graham-mlk-civil-rights.
91. David L. Chappell, 2004, *A Stone of Hope: Prophetic Religion and the Death of Jim Crow,* University of North Carolina Press, 141.
92. Tisby, *Color of Compromise,* 134–35.
93. Chappell, *Stone of Hope,* 142.
94. Gilbreath, "Billy Graham Had a Dream."
95. Martin, *Prophet with Honor,* 301–2.
96. Chappell, *Stone of Hope,* 143.
97. Kidd, *Who Is an Evangelical?,* 101.

98. Billy Graham, October 4, 1993, "Racism and the Evangelical Church," *Christianity Today*, christianitytoday.com/1993/10/myth-of-racial-progress.
99. Jay Reeves, February 25, 2018, "Billy Graham Had Pride and Regret on Civil Rights Issues," *The Associated Press*, apnews.com/article/20d646efe23c469fbbc83cd04ec2fc17.
100. Blake, "Where Billy Graham 'Missed the Mark.'"
101. John 8:11, KJV.
102. Pannell, *My Friend, the Enemy*, 65.
103. Justin Giboney, interview by Bonnie Kristian, August 28, 2025.
104. Rachel Gilson, interview by Bonnie Kristian, September 16, 2025.
105. Lilly Sullivan, April 19, 2019, "The Sudden Departure," *This American Life*, thisamericanlife.org/673/transcript.
106. Ruth Graham, September 22, 2024, "What Happened When an Ohio Megachurch Decided to Tackle Racism," *The New York Times*, nytimes.com/2024/09/22/books/review/undivided-hahrie-han.html.
107. Carrie McKean, August 30, 2023, "My Pastor Friend Likes Trump's Border Policy. He Also Shelters Migrants," *Christianity Today*, christianitytoday.com/2023/08/pastor-trump-border-policy-migrant-asylum-shelter-texas.
108. Silliman, interview.
109. Yonat Shimron, August 21, 2025, "Samaritan's Purse Joins Gaza Humanitarian Foundation's Aid Efforts in Gaza," *Religion News Service*, religionnews.com/2025/08/21/samaritans-purse-joins-gaza-humanitarian-foundations-aid-efforts-in-gaza/.
110. Wehner, "Where Did Evangelicals Go Wrong?"
111. Douthat, *Bad Religion*, 204.
112. Diana Chandler, December 12, 2024, "Christians Are Most Charitable; Giving Drives Happiness, State of the Bible Finds," *Baptist Press*, baptistpress.com/resource-library/news/christians-are-most-charitable-giving-drives-happiness-state-of-the-bible-finds.
113. Karl Zinsmeister, 2019, "Less God, Less Giving?" *Philanthropy Magazine*, philanthropyroundtable.org/magazine/less-god-less-giving.
114. Ryan Burge, September 4, 2024, "White evangelicals [clearly] stand apart when it comes [to] their views of the aim of the church. 59% of them say that God is more concerned about individual

morality than social inequalities. It's ~30% of other Christian groups," *X*, x.com/ryanburge/status/1830945055944609894.

115. James 3:9–10.
116. Edward Gilbreath, email, November 1, 2025.
117. Alberta, *Kingdom, the Power, and the Glory*, 12–13.
118. Gilbreath, email.
119. Wear, interview.
120. Luke 18:11.
121. Colossians 1:9–10.
122. Kidd, *Who Is an Evangelical?*, 122.
123. Alberta, *Kingdom, the Power, and the Glory*, 135: "This, Vincent Bacote told me, is what's absent inside much of the American evangelical Church. 'If you ask me what's the biggest problem with evangelicalism, I'd say it's a catechesis problem. It's a formation problem, a discipleship problem. These are people who are supposed to have a knowledge of the Bible, but many of them don't,' said Bacote, a renowned theologian on the Wheaton faculty. 'The genius of evangelicalism is the breadth of it. The hazard is the lack of depth. A lot of these people are just not going deep enough.' By remaining shallow in the scriptures, Bacote said, too many American Christians have avoided a necessary showdown between their own base cultural proclivities and God's perfect standard. When Christians are discipled primarily by society, inevitably they look to scripture for affirmation of their habits and behaviors and political views. 'But if the Bible is the word of God, then God ought to be interrogating those things. That's why Jesus came: to fix your vertical relationship with God,' Bacote said. 'He wants your whole life. He wants to transform who you are.' "
124. Ross Douthat, February 29, 2016, "A thought sent back in time to the theocracy panic of 2005: If you dislike the religious right, wait till you meet the post-religious right," *X*, x.com/DouthatNYT/status/704462319074594816.
125. Daniel K. Williams, August 2, 2022, "White Southern Evangelicals Are Leaving the Church," *Christianity Today*, christianitytoday.com/2022/08/church-attendance-sbc-southern-evangelicals-now-lapsed: "To be sure, the majority of Southern white churches have encouraged the Republican political ideology that contributed to Donald Trump's election as president and the maintenance of struc-

tural racism. But at the same time, even the most politically conservative churches have promoted a sense of community that encourages people to be concerned for others and trusting of them. They have encouraged sexual fidelity and have frowned on self-indulgence, especially when it comes to alcohol and marijuana. When people leave church, they retain that moralism—at least insofar as it pertains to other people—but lose the sense of self-sacrifice and trust in others. They keep their Bible, their gun, their pro-life pin, and their MAGA hat, but also pick up a condom and a marijuana joint and lose whatever willingness they had to care for other people in community. For decades, many pundits have warned about the political dangers of a Southern Christian Right that was intent on blurring the boundaries of church and state. But whatever those dangers might have been, perhaps the greater threat to democracy in the South right now is a de-churched populist Right that is just as angry about efforts to correct racial injustice and even more individualistic."

126. Giboney, interview.

CHAPTER FOUR

1. Washington State Department of Licensing, 2026, "Change your gender designation," dol.wa.gov/driver-licenses-and-permits/update-driver-license-information/change-your-gender-designation.
2. United States Court of Appeals for the Ninth Circuit, May 29, 2025, "Olympus Spa v. Armstrong," *United States Courts,* cdn.ca9.uscourts.gov/datastore/opinions/2025/05/29/23-4031.pdf, 12.
3. Ipsos, January 10, 2025, "New York Times/Ipsos Survey," *The New York Times,* static01.nyt.com/newsgraphics/documenttools/f548560f100205ef/e656ddda-full.pdf, 14.
4. Sun Lee, interview by Bonnie Kristian, October 23, 2025.
5. Stephen L. Carter, 1994, *The Culture of Disbelief: How American Law and Politics Trivialize Religious Devotion,* Anchor Books, 3. See also 4–12.
6. Carter, *Culture of Disbelief,* 8, 9.
7. Carter, *Culture of Disbelief,* 23–25.
8. C. Smith, *American Evangelicalism,* 184–86.
9. Butler, *White Evangelical Racism,* 131.
10. George Yancey, 2015, *Hostile Environment: Understanding and Responding to Anti-Christian Bias,* InterVarsity Press, 42.
11. Yancey, *Hostile Environment,* 43.

12. Douthat, *Bad Religion,* 72–73: "In the early years of the sexual revolution it was easy for many Americans, most of whom still considered themselves good Christians, to decide that their faith's sexual ethic wasn't just outdated—it was repressive, cruel, and pernicious, meant, in turn, that anyone who defended it must be either nostalgic for an age of sexual repression or else a helpless victim of false consciousness, unable to escape the burden of shame and guilt a religious upbringing had imposed. Over time, this premise would become perhaps the biggest drag on Christianity's public credibility. It created a presumptive bias against the Christian position on sexual ethics, no matter what arguments were deployed on its behalf. (If you opposed abortion, you wanted to control women. If you were against gay marriage, you were probably a pathetic closet case yourself. If you held up monogamy and fidelity as high ideals, it was just because you couldn't get laid.)"
13. Yancey, *Hostile Environment,* 43.
14. Carter, *Culture of Disbelief,* 22.
15. Rachel Weiner, June 11, 2020, "Political and Health Leaders' Embrace of Floyd Protests Fuels Debate over Coronavirus Restrictions," *The Washington Post,* washingtonpost.com/health/political-and-health-leaders-embrace-of-floyd-protests-fuels-debate-over-coronavirus-restrictions/2020/06/11/9c60bca6-a761-11ea-bb20-ebf0921f3bbd_story.html.
16. Michael Brendan Dougherty, July 8, 2020, "The question is whether a positive law of equality, and a religious autonomous zone of negative religious liberty is practicable. The inevitable hospital cases are going to tell us a great deal," *X,* x.com/michaelbd/status/1280872365489106944.
17. Romans 12:1.
18. Cindy Wooden, August 25, 2025, "Authentic Faith Is Seen in Love of God and Neighbor, Pope Says," *United States Conference of Catholic Bishops,* usccb.org/news/2025/authentic-faith-seen-love-god-and-neighbor-pope-says.
19. Acts 5:29.
20. Miroslav Volf, March 10, 2022, "On Private Christianity," *The Centre for Public Christianity,* publicchristianity.org/video/on-private-christianity.
21. Billy Binion, June 3, 2025, "Female Nude Spa in Washington Can't Bar Transgender Clients with Male Genitalia, Federal Court Rules,"

Reason, reason.com/2025/06/03/female-nude-spa-in-washington-cant-bar-transgender-clients-with-male-genitalia-federal-court-rules/?nab=1.

22. Olympus Spa, "Spa Entry Policy," *Olympus Spa,* olympusspa.com/lynnwood/spa-entry-policy.
23. Lee, interview.
24. Lee, interview.
25. Binion, "Female Nude Spa in Washington."
26. Josh Blackman, March 12, 2026, "Judge VanDyke: 'This is a case about swinging dicks,'" *The Volokh Conspiracy,* reason.com/volokh/2026/03/12/judge-vandyke-this-is-a-case-about-swinging-dicks.
27. United States Court of Appeals for the Ninth Circuit, "Olympus Spa v. Armstrong," 19–20, internal citations deleted for clarity.
28. United States Court of Appeals for the Ninth Circuit, "Olympus Spa v. Armstrong," 21–24.
29. Lexi, Meagan, and Kyle, interview.
30. Lee, interview.
31. Carter, *Culture of Disbelief,* 23–25.
32. Douthat, *Bad Religion,* 71–72.
33. Angie Schwartz and Kevin Gaines, November 14, 2024, "All County Letter No. 24–69," *California Department of Social Services,* cdss.ca.gov/Portals/9/Additional-Resources/Letters-and-Notices/ACLs/2024/24-69.pdf?ver=2024-11-19-154231-617.
34. Emily Baumgaertner Nunn, October 26, 2025, "Can Anyone Rescue the Trafficked Girls of L.A.'s Figueroa Street?" *The New York Times,* nytimes.com/2025/10/26/magazine/sex-trafficking-girls-la-figueroa.html.
35. Renn, *Life in the Negative World,* 6–7.
36. Renn, *Life in the Negative World,* 4–5, 35.
37. Renn, *Life in the Negative World,* 195.
38. Schwartz and Gaines, "All County Letter No. 24–69."
39. Renn, *Life in the Negative World,* 79.
40. Alberta, *Kingdom, the Power, and the Glory,* 121–22.
41. Bonnie Kristian, November 19, 2020, "American Politics Is Fundamentally Unserious About Christianity," *The Week,* theweek.com/articles/950623/american-politics-fundamentally-unserious-about-christianity.

42. Worthen, interview.
43. Michael Kinsley, February 19, 2001, "Don't Want to Convert? Just Say No," *Time,* content.time.com/time/subscriber/article/0,33009,999239,00.html.
44. Renn, *Life in the Negative World,* 125.
45. Rachel Gilson, October 2017, "I Never Became Straight. Perhaps That Was Never God's Goal," *Christianity Today,* christianitytoday.com/2017/09/i-never-became-straight-perhaps-that-was-never-gods-goal.
46. Gilson, interview.
47. Tertullian, 1885, "The Chaplet, or De Corona," *New Advent,* newadvent.org/fathers/0304.htm.

CHAPTER FIVE

1. Andrew L. Whitehead and Samuel L. Perry, 2022, *Taking America Back for God: Christian Nationalism in the United States,* Oxford University Press, 7–8.
2. Whitehead and Perry, *Taking America Back for God,* 9.
3. Philip S. Gorski and Samuel L. Perry, 2022, *The Flag and the Cross: White Christian Nationalism and the Threat to American Democracy,* Oxford University Press, 4, 17. See also 5–7.
4. Antonio and Jane, interview.
5. Whitehead and Perry, *Taking America Back for God,* 98–99.
6. Antonio and Jane, interview.
7. Antonio, email, November 12, 2025.
8. Antonio and Jane, interview.
9. Kidd, *Who Is an Evangelical?,* 91–92.
10. Douthat, *Bad Religion,* 3.
11. Carter, *The Culture of Disbelief,* 38.
12. Chris Hedges, 2006, *American Fascists: The Christian Right and the War on America,* Free Press, 26–27.
13. Hedges, *American Fascists,* 36–37: "The radical Christian Right must be forced to include other points of view to counter their hate talk in their own broadcasts, watched by tens of millions of Americans. They must be denied the right to demonize whole segments of American society, saying they are manipulated by Satan and worthy only of conversion or eradication. They must be made to treat their

opponents with respect and acknowledge the right of a fair hearing even as they exercise their own freedom to disagree with their opponents."

14. Yancey, *Hostile Environment,* 19–20.
15. Sarah Jones, December 6, 2023, "America's White Evangelical Problem," *New York,* nymag.com/intelligencer/2023/12/tim-alberta-book-review-americas-white-evangelical-problem.html.
16. Whitehead and Perry, *Taking America Back for God,* 126.
17. Whitehead and Perry, *Taking America Back for God,* 138.
18. Whitehead and Perry, *Taking America Back for God,* 42.
19. Charles Taylor, 2014, "How to Define Secularism," in *Boundaries of Toleration,* ed. Charles Taylor and Alfred Stepan, Columbia University Press, 72: "There are zones of a secular state in which the language used has to be neutral. But these do not include citizen deliberation, as Rawls at first thought, or even deliberation in the legislature, as Habermas seems to think from the lines I have quoted. This zone can be described as the official language of the state: the language in which legislation, administrative decrees, and court judgments must be couched. It is self-evident that a law before Parliament couldn't contain a justifying clause of the type 'Whereas the Bible tells us that p.' And the same goes, mutatis mutandis, for the justification of a judicial decision in the court's verdict. But this has nothing to do with the specific nature of religious language. It would be equally improper to have a legislative clause: 'Whereas Marx has shown that religion is the opium of the people' or 'Whereas Kant has shown that the only thing good without qualification is a good will.' The grounds for both these kinds of exclusions is the neutrality of the state. The state can be neither Christian nor Muslim nor Jewish, but by the same token it should also be neither Marxist nor Kantian, nor Utilitarian. Of course, the democratic state will end up voting for laws that (in the best case) reflect the actual convictions of its citizens, which will be either Christian or Muslim, etc., through the whole gamut of views held in a modern society. But the decisions can't be framed in a way that gives special recognition to one of these views. This is not easy to do; the lines are hard to draw, and they must always be drawn anew. But such is the nature of the enterprise that is the modern secular state. And what better alternative is there for diverse democracies?"
20. Butler, *White Evangelical Racism,* 70.

21. Brad East, July 4, 2022, "Another Option for Christian Politics," *Front Porch Republic,* frontporchrepublic.com/2022/07/another-option-for-christian-politics.
22. Yancey, *Hostile Environment,* 25.
23. Katherine Stewart, 2025, *Money, Lies, and God: Inside the Movement to Destroy American Democracy,* Bloomsbury, 13.
24. Stewart, *Money, Lies, and God,* 12.
25. Katherine Stewart, 2019, *The Power Worshippers: Inside the Dangerous Rise of Religious Nationalism,* Bloomsbury, 3–4.
26. Stewart, *Power Worshippers,* 3–4.
27. Stewart, *Power Worshippers,* 248, 256–61.
28. *The Gospel Coalition,* thegospelcoalition.org.
29. American Anglican Council, "What Portion of the Anglican Communion Does GAFCON and the GSFA Represent?" *Anglican Perspectives,* americananglican.org/what-portion-of-the-anglican-communion-does-gafcon-and-the-gsfa-represent.
30. "Primates Council & Advisors," GAFCON, americananglican.org/what-portion-of-the-anglican-communion-does-gafcon-and-the-gsfa-represent.
31. Stewart, *Power Worshippers,* 258, 260.
32. "Engel v. Vitale," *Oyez,* oyez.org/cases/1961/468.
33. Whitehead and Perry, *Taking America Back for God,* 33–34.
34. Whitehead and Perry, *Taking America Back for God,* 41–42.
35. Pew Research Center, October 27, 2022, "45% of Americans Say U.S. Should Be a 'Christian Nation,'" *Pew Research Center,* pewresearch.org/religion/2022/10/27/45-of-americans-say-u-s-should-be-a-christian-nation: "While some people who say the U.S. should be a Christian nation define the concept as one where a nation's laws are based on Christian tenets and the nation's leaders are Christian, it is much more common for people in this category to see a Christian nation as one where people are more broadly guided by Christian values or a belief in God, even if its laws are not explicitly Christian and its leaders can have a variety of faiths or no faith at all. Some people who say the U.S. should be a Christian nation are thinking about the religious makeup of the population; to them, a Christian nation is a country where most people are Christians. Others are simply envisioning a place where people treat each other well and have good morals."

36. Whitehead and Perry, *Taking America Back for God*, 40–41.
37. Whitehead and Perry, *Taking America Back for God*, xv–xvi.
38. Gorski and Perry, *Flag and the Cross*, 100–101.
39. Marshal Cohen, February 27, 2021, "Trump supporters who breached the Capitol: 'It was not Antifa,'" CNN, cnn.com/2021/02/27/politics/capitol-attack-trump-supporters-not-antifa.
40. Matthew D. Taylor, 2024, *The Violent Take It by Force: The Christian Movement That Is Threatening Our Democracy*, Broadleaf, 3.
41. M. Taylor, *Violent Take It by Force*, 148–49.
42. M. Taylor, *Violent Take It by Force*, 3, 195.
43. M. Taylor, *Violent Take It by Force*, 195, 249. See also 226–28.
44. M. Taylor, *Violent Take It by Force*, 148–49.
45. Tom Skinner, 1970, "The U.S. Racial Crisis and World Evangelism (1970)," *InterVarsity Christian Fellowship*, web.archive.org/web/20150411074435/https://urbana.org/transcript/us-racial-crisis-and-world-evangelism-1970.
46. Edward Gilbreath, September 16, 1996, "A Prophet out of Harlem," *Christianity Today*, christianitytoday.com/1996/09/prophet-out-of-harlem.
47. Skinner, "U.S. Racial Crisis and World Evangelism (1970)."
48. Skinner, "U.S. Racial Crisis and World Evangelism (1970)."
49. Isaiah 11:1–9; Matthew 12:25–28; John 18:36.
50. Whitehead and Perry, *Taking America Back for God*, 4–5.
51. Ryan Burge, February 22, 2024, "Has Christian Nationalism Intensified or Faded?" *Graphs About Religion*, www.graphsaboutreligion.com/p/has-christian-nationalism-intensified.
52. Ryan Burge, email, November 13, 2025.
53. Baylor Religion Survey, 2025, "The Values and Beliefs of the American Public Survey—A National Study," baylorreligionsurvey.research.baylor.edu/sites/g/files/ecbvkj1931/files/2025-11/Wave%20VII%20BRS%20Survey%20Questions.pdf, 6.
54. Baylor Religion Survey, 2025, "Wave VII—2025 Survey," baylorreligionsurvey.research.baylor.edu/wave-vii-2025-survey.
55. David Gilbert and Tess Owen, November 8, 2022, "Meet the 'Black Robe Regiment' of Extremist Pastors Spreading Christian Nationalism," *Vice*, vice.com/en/article/who-are-the-black-robe-regiment.
56. Grant Wacker, interview by Bonnie Kristian, October 1, 2025.

57. Barack Obama, June 28, 2006, "'Call to Renewal' Keynote Address," *Barack Obama (accessed via Internet Archive),* web.archive.org/web/2008 0131044053/http://obama.senate.gov/speech/060628-call_to _renewal.

CONCLUSION

1. Brad and Angela, interview by Bonnie Kristian, October 26, 2025.
2. Brad and Angela, interview.
3. Silliman, interview.
4. Nathan O. Hatch, 1989, *The Democratization of American Christianity,* Yale University Press, 216.
5. Credit to Daniel Silliman for this analogy. Quote via Tom Huizenga and Ashalen Sims, February 24, 2011, "Sing Out Mr. President: Bill Clinton's Proverb of Wrong and Right," *NPR,* npr.org/sections /deceptivecadence/2011/02/28/133973258/sing-out-mr-president -bill-clintons-proverb-of-wrong-and-right.
6. Hebrews 13:8.
7. 1 Timothy 1:15.
8. Romans 5:10; 1 Corinthians 15:26; Colossians 1:15–22; Hebrews 2:14–15.
9. Romans 12; Hebrews 10:19–25; James 2:14–26.
10. Milliner, interview.

ABOUT THE AUTHOR

BONNIE KRISTIAN is deputy editor at *Christianity Today* and author of *Untrustworthy* and *A Flexible Faith.* She is a fellow at Defense Priorities, a foreign policy think tank. Her writing on evangelicalism, the modern American right, foreign policy, civil liberties, and electoral politics has been widely published. Bonnie Kristian is a graduate of Bethel Seminary with a master of arts in Christian Thought. She lives in Pittsburgh with her husband and their three children.